BOOK CARD

PLEASE KEEP THIS CARD

IN BOOK POCKET

A CHARGE WILL BE MADE IF
THIS CARD IS NOT WITH THE
BOOK WHEN RETURNED.

LOS ANGELES PUBLIC LIBRARY

PH

A

000895

SERMONS 0 001

IC SERMONS

RIST

---

31 845360010   PH
232.921 C6145

CLASSIC SERMONS ON THE BIRTH
OF CHRIST
                          000895

DO NOT REMOVE FORMS FROM POCKET

CARD OWNER IS RESPONSIBLE FOR ALL
LIBRARY MATERIAL ISSUED ON HIS CARD

PREVENT DAMAGE - A charge is made for
damage to this item or the forms in the pocket.

RETURN ITEMS PROMPTLY - A fine is charged for
each day an item is overdue, including Sundays
and holidays.

REPORT A LOST ITEM AT ONCE - The charge for
a lost item includes the cost of the item plus a
$5.00 non-refundable service fee.

AUG 11   LOS ANGELES PUBLIC LIBRARY

CLASSIC SERMONS
ON THE
BIRTH OF CHRIST

CLASSIC SERMONS
ON THE
BIRTH OF CHRIST

KREGEL PUBLICATIONS
Grand Rapids, Michigan 49501

Classic Sermons on the Birth of Christ, compiled by Warren
W. Wiersbe. © 1991 by Kregel Publications, a division of
Kregel, Inc., P. O. Box 2607, Grand Rapids, MI 49501. All
rights reserved.

Cover Photo: Westminster Presbyterian Church,
                Grand Rapids, Michigan
Cover Design: Don Ellens

Library of Congress Cataloging-in-Publication Data

Classic Sermons on the Birth of Christ / compiled
by Warren W. Wiersbe.
      p.   cm.— (Kregel classic sermons series)
   Includes index.

   1. Christmas Sermons. 2. Sermons, American.
3. Sermons, English. I. Wiersbe, Warren W. II. Series:
Kregel classic sermons series.

BV4257.C57   1991   252'.61—dc20   91-11816
                                                       CIP
ISBN   0-8254-4044-0 (pbk.)

            1 2 3 4 5 Printing/Year 95 94 93 92 91

Printed in the United States of America

CONTENTS

5

SCRIPTURE TEXT INDEX

PREFACE

THE *KREGEL CLASSIC SERMONS SERIES* is an attempt to assemble and publish meaningful sermons from master preachers about significant themes.

These are *sermons*, not essays or chapters taken from books about themes. Not all of these sermons could be called "great," but all of them are *meaningful*. They apply the truths of the Bible to the needs of the human heart, which is something that all effective preaching must do.

While some are better known than others, all of the preachers, whose sermons I have selected, had important ministries and were highly respected in their day. The fact that a sermon is included in this volume does not mean that either the compiler or the publisher agrees with or endorses everything that the man did, preached, or wrote. The sermon is here because it has a valued contribution to make.

These are sermons about *significant* themes. The pulpit is no place to play with trivia. The preacher has thirty minutes in which to help mend broken hearts, change defeated lives, and save lost souls; and he can never accomplish this demanding ministry by distribu-ting homiletical tidbits. In these difficult days, we do not need "clever" pulpiteers who discuss the times; we need dedicated ambassadors who will preach the eternities.

The reading of these sermons can enrich your own spiritual life. The studying of them can enrich your own skills as an interpreter and expounder of God's truth. However God uses these sermons in your own life and ministry, my prayer is that His Church around the world will be encouraged and strengthened.

WARREN W. WIERSBE

The Secret of Peace and Goodwill

John Henry Jowett (1864-1923) was known as "the greatest preacher in the English-speaking world." Born in Yorkshire, England, he was ordained into the Congregational ministry. His second pastorate was at the famous Carr's Lane Church, Birmingham, where he followed the eminent Dr. Robert W. Dale. From 1911-18, he pastored the Fifth Avenue Presbyterian Church, New York City; and from 1918-23, he ministered at Westminster Chapel, London, succeeding G. Campbell Morgan. He wrote many books of devotional messages and sermons. This message was preached at Westminster Chapel, London, on December 25, 1918, and was published by The Westminster Chapel Bookstall in their monthly sermon series. I do not believe this message is found in Jowett's published sermons or in any sermon anthology.

John Henry Jowett

1

THE SECRET OF PEACE AND GOODWILL

And suddenly there was with the angel a multitude of the heavenly host praising God, and saying, Glory to God in the highest, and on earth peace, goodwill toward men (Luke 2:13,14).

WHAT UNEARTHLY MUSIC in times like these! How remote it all appears! How dreamlike! How unreal! It has the same sort of incongruity as if we were to come upon a scrap of fair legend, or a touch of ancient romance, in one of the columns of our daily paper which was describing the horrors of a battlefield in Flanders. To hear the angel-music just now is like finding a quaint bit of medievalism in a bustling thoroughfare of modern New York. The angel-music seems out of place. We have almost forgotten the heavenly strains in the harsh and brutal antagonism of immediate events. To listen to the angels just now—it is as though the carol singers are at our door, and while they are singing outside the house a fierce quarrel is going on inside. And some people are thinking, and some people are saying, "The old song is a fond illusion! It is an old song, and nothing more! Its peaceful vision is a mirage! Its fair promise is a baseless dream! The music has no background in reality! It mocks where it used to comfort, and it irritates where it used to inspire!" That is what many people are thinking, and what some people are saying. And therefore it might be well to listen to the angels again, as the music comes to us through these two thousand years; "Glory to God in the highest, and on earth peace, goodwill among men."

And that is all an illusion, is it? "Yes, where is the promised peace? Where is the goodwill among men? Look around and see the irony of reality in the happenings of the whole world!" And one is obliged to admit that peace seems to have been scared into hiding, and goodwill does not appear to have woven many strands in the intimate web of human fraternity. But is there any explanation of the apparent illusion? Has any vital factor been omitted, which may account for the dismal failure? The peace was promised; the goodwill was proclaimed. Is it possible that we may have overlooked something which is altogether imperative if the gracious issues are to be realized? I ask these questions with all the more urgency because I know how prone we are, in other matters than those which are distinctly religious, to fasten our attention on effects, and to be strangely negligent of the causes. Or we fix our gaze upon secondary and subordinate causes and we neglect those that are primary. We hop over essentials; we concentrate our interest on the middle term, or upon the ultimate term, and we ignore the first term, the term which is elemental, fundamental, alphabetic, and fontal. We begin at the wrong place. We take up our position at a point some way down the river, but we will not go up to the springs. We stand where the mighty stream must empty its floods into the ocean, but we will not climb to the great gathering grounds where the floods were born, in the kingdom of cloud and mist, the realm of rain, and snow, and drenching dew.

The Unfinished Song

And so I am wondering whether we may have done this with the angels' song. Have we overlooked any part of it which may be vital to all the rest? Have we accepted one part but ignored another? I am wondering if our emphasis is altogether right and true, or whether a mistaken emphasis may be responsible for all our spiritual poverty and defeat. I turn, therefore, to the angels' song, in order that I may examine its contents, and I am amazed at what seems to be a common omission. Men are everywhere saying or thinking, "Where is the goodwill among men? Where is the peace on earth that was promised?" Yes, but go on with your questions. You have not finished the song. You have left out its initial and primary note. I must finish your series of questions, and I must be allowed to ask, "Where is the glory to God in the highest?" We have fixed our eyes upon the third phrase of the angels' song,—"goodwill among men"; or upon the second phrase,—"peace on earth!" And we have overlooked the first phrase, the phrase which is casual and causative—"glory to God in the highest." That is to say, we have begun at the end, and left out the beginning. We have been concerned about fruits, but we have been careless about roots. If you will really think about the matter, it is clear that we have been wanting rivers to arise without any gathering grounds or springs. That is the explanation of our disillusionment. We have laid hold of the chain at the second link, or the third link, and we have strangely overlooked the first. I want to repeat my words, we have begun at the wrong end, and we have forgotten the beginning. We have been looking for magic harvests. We have been wanting the corn before we had got the field. We have been expecting man to be right with man before man was right with God. We have been looking for harvests, and we have foolishly assumed that harvests would grow out of nothing. We have taken one part of the angels' song and we have thrown away the other. We have ignored the field, and we have then marveled that there was no harvest. For what is the angels' song, in all its harmonious completeness? This the song: "Glory to God in the highest, and on earth peace, goodwill among men."

Now it may be worthwhile to reason about this matter a little more closely. And let us begin here. Peace is not an independent birth. Peace is not a detached creation, unrelated to everything else. Peace is bound up with other things, and is entirely dependent upon them. Peace is the fruit of certain relations, and if those relations are secured peace is inevitable. Let us look at one or two analogies in quite different spheres. Take for illustration what I might be permitted to call architectural peace. Architectural peace is just the serenity of a structure which stands firm, quiet, and untrembling in the fiercest blast. That architectural serenity, that quietude of material fellowship, stone with stone, and timber with timber, is dependent upon more important relations. Those more important relations are determined by the perpendicular, and the spirit-level, and the plumb-line. That is to say, if the architect is to endow a building with peace he must first endow it with rectitude. Architectural peace is not a direct creation; it is the inevitable fruit of other conditions, in which certain laws are most scrupulously obeyed.

Musical Peace

Or take what I may call musical peace. Musical peace is not silence, it is harmony. And here again the pleasing concord is the happy issue of other relations which are paramount and primary. Let one string of a violin be out of statutory relationship with the other strings, and nothing that you can possibly do will result in musical power, and sweetness, and peace. Let one string of the instrument be tense, let another be lax, let another be broken, and where is your chance of harmony? Where is the possibility of melodious peace? We cannot have musical peace unless the instrument is in tune. Our instrument must be adjusted before its sounds can be in concord. And therefore it is imperative that we attend to the primary relations of the violin if we would have harmonious creations. That is to say, the concord is the second term, and the adjustment is the first.

Bodily Peace

And so it is with bodily peace, which is physical health. The peace of the body, in which no organ is presumptuous or aggressive, is not an immediate creation. It is a secondary creation, resulting from the right relationships of all the members of the body. Even in the body there must be physical rectitude before there can be physical peace. If the members of the body are not in their appointed relations there will be organic tumult and strife. So that in the bodily life, if we would secure peace, we must first of all secure adjustment.

All these illustrations have one significance; if we would have peace in any one of these realms we must begin further back, and start with the relationships out of which peace is born. And so it is with the supreme peace of which the angels sang, the peace of human concord, which is appointed to be the music of the body corporate, the harmony of the entire family of man. Peace is the outcome of certain relationships, and when those relationships are secured the peace is assured.

You will find this teaching everywhere in the Word of God, and everywhere it is given first place. Listen to a few examples which might be indefinitely multiplied; "Thou wilt keep him in perfect peace whose mind is stayed on Thee"; "Righteousness and peace have kissed each other"; "Great peace have they who love Thy law"; "Wherefore, being justified by faith, we have peace." In every one of these scriptural passages, and in a thousand more, peace is declared to be not a root but a fruit, the fruit of personal rightness with God. And that is where the angels' song began, the song which was sung to the shepherds below the village of Bethlehem. It began not with goodwill among men, not with peace on earth, but with that which will be productive of these, as surely as the sun is the father of lights. The angels' song begins with "Glory to God in the highest." And, therefore, I must ask myself, in these gloomy and distressing days through which we are passing, days which are darkened with human hatred, and ill-will, and racial warfare, and strife—where do / my thinking begin? Does it begin in secondary things, / even in the tertiary things, or does it begin in the ꞁmary? Does it begin where the angels' song began, ꞁ "Glory to God in the highest," in the rectification of tꞁ ꞁ supreme relationship, in the reconciliation and adjustment of God and man? If only we would give glory to God in the highest, peace on earth is sure, and goodwill among men is secured.

A Vital Relationship

But what is the relationship which gives glory to God in the highest? There are many ways in which we can be related to God, but only one of them is vital. All the other relationships might be described as contacts, but they are not communions. They have external connections but they are not pervaded by the commerce of vital fellowship. For instance there is the philosophic relationship, which is merely the mental acceptance of certain theories of being. There is the theological relationship, which is the entertainment and perhaps the championship of certain creeds, a championship which may be accompanied by great fervor and even ferocity. There is the ecclesiastical relationship, which is just a formal entry in the register of the Church's roll, and may indicate no more vital communion with the eternal God than the writing of your name in the callers' book at Buckingham Palace would denote that you were a bosom friend of the King. And there are other conventional relationships which one might name; there is the governmental relationship which stamps the name of God upon its coins, or inserts a respectful phrase in its laws, or introduces the divine name into its documents—all of which may have no more to do with the living God than the waterlines on my notepaper have to do with the nobility or the ignominy of my life.

All these relationships to God are formal, nominal, literal. They are not vital, and they do not give vital glory to God. How then can one come into a vital relationship with God, into such a relationship as will give God glory, and out of which all other forms of rectitude will spring, as surely as the waving corn springs from the fertile field? How can we get right with God with the rightness which will make us right with man? That is the question of questions even in this distracting day. The biggest thing you and I can think about in all the confusion of our time is how we can all get right with God. How can we give such glory to God that the glory will create peace on earth and goodwill among men? He Whose birth we celebrate today gave us the all-sufficient clue. Christ Jesus said, "I am the way!" To get into right relationships with Christ is to be in right relationships with God. And what sort of relationship does Jesus Christ demand when He speaks to the souls of men? There is no uncertainty about the response. Christ Jesus asks for the full surrender of our life to the governance of His will, and to the power of His saving grace. He calls us first of all to bring our life and offer it to Him as our Savior, and then, secondly, to use that offered life in obedience to our Lord.

And, my brethren, we cannot do that as races or as peoples or as nationalities or as crowds. In these matters we get nowhere if we begin with mobs and millions. It is the surrender of the personal life to a personal Lord and Savior. I have no confidence in anything else. Unless the end of the war brings us nearer to this consummation we are going to begin once more treading the darkening way of suspicion and misunderstanding and moral defeat. I devoutly hope that the League of Peace among the nations will be established, but the best work that League will do will be only external, secondary and subordinate. Vital peace among men is to be brought about by the individual man being at peace with God—rectified and justified and sanctified in the power of God's redeeming love and grace. We simply cannot save the world in masses. We cannot, by any leagues and treaties, bring the world into congenial and fraternal peace. Salvation and peace are to be found only in the surrender of the personal life to the Savior-hood and comradeship of Christ. True life begins where the saints have always begun, and where every pilgrim has begun who became a chivalrous Greatheart on life's way. True life begins here, and the new world will begin here,—

"Rock of Ages, cleft for me,
Let me hide myself in Thee."

It Must Begin With Me

No, we cannot be saved in masses. The organ-builder cannot tune the organ in the mass. We should have nothing to do with any man who came with a theory of collectivism to the general repair of the organ. Each individual note has to be rectified, and out of the rectified individuals the organ-builder gets his harmonious unity. Except a note be born again it cannot enter into the kingdom of harmony. "Except a *man* be born again he cannot enter the *kingdom*." We begin with the *man* in the formation of the *kingdom*. The reborn men make the heavenly kingdom.

When a man is born the kingdom begins, and as men are born the kingdom comes. That is the first relation in the holy sequence. Man surrenders his life to the glory of God. That is the first phase of the angels' song, "Glory to God in the highest!" The individual man right with the highest! Then will come peace on earth and goodwill among men. The angels' song begins with "Glory to God"; it ends with "Goodwill among men." First glory, then peace! That is the Christmas music! And that is Christianity!

How think you then? Is the angels' song an illusion? Has it mocked the world by the falsity of its promise? Has Christianity failed? Has its purposed ministry turned out to be only a tinted bubble? Or have all the fearful events of our time only given a terrible proof that the teachings of the angels' songs are true, and that they cannot be ignored with impunity? Christianity says, "You cannot have peace by merely saying, "Lord, Lord!" Has that been proved to be true or false? Christianity says, "A professing Christian who does not live in Christ Jesus is cast forth as a branch and is withered." Has that been proved to be true or false? Christianity says, "You cannot have outward harmony and inner discord! You cannot have external rectitude with internal crookedness! If you forsake the perpendicular you will have a bulging wall!" Is that being proved to be true or false? Christianity says, "You cannot have peace on earth and goodwill among men if men are disrupted from God and living in alienation from His holy fellowship." Is that being proved to be true or false?

Christianity says, "When lives are surrendered to the saving grace and power of Christ there is spiritual vitality and moral nobility, and the Christian spirit is incarnated in every part of their communion." Is that being proved to be true or false? What say you, has Christianity failed? There is a much more pressing question. Has Christianity been tried? We have been trying to gather harvests before we have got the field, and we have tragically failed. We have been trying to organize peace and goodwill as though it were a manufactured product, and we have pitiably failed. We have tried to arrange fraternity round a council-table, and we have miserably failed. And now, brethren, suppose we try Christ! And suppose we begin where the angels' song began, by giving glory to God in the highest! Suppose we glorify God by the full surrender of our lives in body, soul, and spirit, to the saving governance and control of the Lord Jesus Christ! We have been looking for grapes and we have not got the Vine. Suppose we now reverse the order; get the Vine and then look for the grapes. That is my Christmas message. First the Vine, then the grapes! First glory to God in the highest, then peace on earth, goodwill among men. And I would to God that everywhere today men and women would hush their strife and hear the angels sing. I would that the angels' song might be heard in every city, and every town, and every village in every land throughout the world. But we must listen to all the song, every part of it! Yes, all the song, root and all, and all in all! "Glory to God in the highest, and on earth peace, goodwill among men."

The Mother of Our Lord

George H. Morrison (1866-1928) assisted the great
Alexander Whyte in Edinburgh, pastored two churches,
and then became pastor in 1902 of the distinguished
Wellington Church on University Avenue in Glasgow. His
preaching drew great crowds; in fact, people had to line
up an hour before the services to be sure to get seats in
the large auditorium. Morrison was a master of the use of
imagination in preaching, yet his messages are solidly
biblical.

This sermon is taken from *Advent and Christmas
Sermons* edited by Frederick J. North and published in
London in 1925 by James Clark and Company.

George H. Morrison

2

THE MOTHER OF OUR LORD

Hail, thou that art highly favored, the Lord is with thee:
blessed art thou among women (Luke 1:28).

AMONG ALL THE influences of home there is none more
powerful than that of motherhood. It is the molding and
inspiring force in tender and impressionable years. "The
hand that rocks the cradle rules the world." In that bold
line there is a deal of truth. The mother's shadow falling
across the cradle is a shadow of blessing or of woe. When
the eyes are opening, when the heart is softest, when the
little will is yet unformed—what tremendous influence
the mother wields. There comes a time with the advance
of years when the impress of the father is determinative.
The strength and masculine energy of fatherhood will be
needed then to guide and to control. But in the opening
days, when the child is but a babe—when life is fresh,
and when the world is wonderful—it is the love of
motherhood more than that of fatherhood that interprets
and conveys the love of God.

Now, if that be so with every infant you may be certain
it was so with Jesus. All that a mother ever meant for
you, that His mother must have meant for Him. He was
born of a woman—made under the law. Did you ever link
these words together? Is not the first law we know in life
the gentle and controlling law of motherhood? And so our
Lord, who on the cross of Calvary fulfilled the eternal law
of God for us, began by obedience to the law of motherhood.
He was as helpless, He was as dependent, as any other
little babe in Nazareth. He hung upon His mother's breast
as really as afterwards He hung upon the Cross. And how
He was molded in these childish years by the love and
sweetness and patience of His mother we shall never
understand, in all its fullness, till we cast our crowns

down at His feet. How could we better spend our Christmas Sunday, then, than by thinking for a little about Mary? It is thus that we can join the angel song, "Hail, thou that art highly favored among women." What do we know of her, what can we learn of her, as we read the simple tale of the evangelist? It is on that I should like to speak.

Her Obscurity

I think the chief thing to impress us about Mary is just the obscurity in which she walks. The days and months and years go hurrying by, and of Mary there is scarce a trace. That our Lord had never ceased to love her tenderly we know from that memorable moment at the Cross. Amid the agonies of that last hour He saw her: "Woman, behold thy son—behold thy mother." And yet, though He had never ceased to love her, and she had never ceased to love her Son, she lives and moves and loves behind a veil. Is it not often so in human life? The things that are dearest are the hidden things. The hands that bless us and the hearts that pray for us are hands and hearts of which the world knows nothing. Happy the life with a background such as that, where there is someone always true and loving, someone whose influence is not less real because it is hidden from the prying eye. Wordsworth has written with infinite contempt of the man who would weep and botanize upon his mother's grave. And a mother's love is like a mother's grave—it is too sacred for the light of day. And that is why Mary in her perfect motherhood is never flaunted on the Gospel page, but moves behind a veil and in obscurity. When one thinks of the place that has been given to Mary in the worship of the Roman Catholic Church; when one thinks of her exalted and conspicuous—the queen of heaven, the celestial rose—one feels that the charm of motherhood is gone. That public throne is not a mother's throne. That glittering crown is not a mother's crown. Motherhood on earth is not like that; neither is perfected motherhood in heaven. All the splendor and show of mariolatry is not half so true to what we know of motherhood as is the sweet obscurity of Scripture.

And yet if we were to think that this obscurity were the

penalty of lack of gifts or character—if we were to think of Mary as a characterless woman, we should be utterly untrue to Scripture. Mary was a woman of a very beautiful character, a woman of a most uncommon nature. There are people of whom you would never hear, though they had the ancestry of David; people predestined to obscurity as others are predestined to renown. She was a woman of most uncommon gifts; with all her quietness she had a strength of character which has got itself written upon the Gospel page.

Think of the journey she took to see her cousin. It was a toilsome and a perilous journey. For a young betrothed maiden such as she was, it was a course of action without precedent. For a Jewish maiden when she was betrothed was not expected to go much abroad; she was expected to stay modestly at home. Here was a woman, then, who had the gift of courage, and with the gift of courage she had the gift of song. Many a mother has the gift of song; Mary had it in preeminence. Here was one of those rare and rounded natures that not only meet life's difficulties bravely, but set the difficulties of the day to music.

Two things always impress me in our Lord: the one is His courage, the other is His poetry. Christ was unfalteringly brave, and yet He was a poet to His fingertips. And it tells us how perfectly He was a human child, drawing His human life from her who bore Him, when these are the qualities we find in Mary. A woman who could act as Mary acted—a woman who could sing as Mary sang—had energy and gifts to make her famous had she any desire to be famous. But Mary had no desire to be famous. She did not want to be the queen of heaven. She wanted to be the mother and the queen of her little growing family at Nazareth.

Her Humility

Now a woman who could so obliterate herself must have been a woman of singular humility. And there are several traces in the narrative that confirm the humility of Mary. Think, for instance, of the Annunciation. There is a picture of the Annunciation, by Rossetti, which I suppose many of you have seen. In it Mary is cowering away, and there is a look of terror in her eyes. But the greatest painters, like Angelico, never paint her with a look like that. They paint her as if she never thought of self at all.

Think of the words that came welling from her heart when she knew she was to be the mother of Messiah. In a single moment she was lifted up into preeminence and immortality. Yet the one thought that rises in her heart is not that she shall be worshiped or admired—"all generations," she says, "shall call me *blessed*." She did not want to be great or to be beautiful—she had no selfish ambitions of that kind. She did not want to have the praise of men, or to be the attraction of a million eyes. Mary's one passion was to be a blessing—Mary's one thought that filled her heart with song was that to weary men and burdened women the world would be different when Christ was born. A woman who could so forget herself was a woman of a singular humility. You will not find her often in the Gospels. She will do nothing to attract attention. For the truest humility is not humiliation, nor any abject disparagement of self. It is never to think about oneself at all.

Her Silence

That being so, we are prepared to learn that Mary was of a meditative nature. Luke tells us twice, as if to fix our thoughts upon it, that she kept things quiet in her heart. Once when the shepherds came with their amazing tidings of the chorus of angels in the sky at Bethlehem; once when the Boy had been lost and then was found in eager converse with the Temple doctors, Luke tells us how Mary kept it in her heart—laid it up there as a secret thing— never breathed a word of it to anybody. Clearly she was a woman who had the gift of silence as truly as she had the gift of song; a woman who knew that there are things you tarnish the moment you begin to speak of them; a woman who set a guard upon her lips—who felt that, without its secret, life was poor—who recognized the indignity of gossiping. There are mothers who can talk of nothing but their children.

Mary was not a mother of that kind. With the most wonderful child that ever a woman nursed, she was silent about Him, and held her peace in Nazareth. She dreamed her dreams, and had her own sweet thoughts, and prayed to God and had her cradle-music—and all the time she kept things in her heart. The beautiful thing is that as her Son grew up, He showed so evidently His mother's influence. You talk of the power of speech our Savior had—have you ever thought of His power of keeping silence? And it seems to me that the reserve of Christ, which added to His authority so mightily, goes back, like His love of the flowers and of the birds, to the days of boyhood in the village home. There is many a son you will never understand unless you know something of his mother. Traits of his character—little compunctions—tendernesses—it is the mother who explains them all. And so in the perfect character of Christ are traits that you can never understand till you remember the motherhood of Mary. When I see Him standing before Pilate; when I find Him refusing to say a single word; when I think how often He was urged to speak and how often he refused to speak; it is then this text comes back to me out of the happy days of home and childhood: "Mary kept all these things within her heart."

Mary's Song

There is another glimpse we get of the Virgin-mother, and we get it in the song she sang. There is one feature of that song you note at once. It is not merely a welling-up of praise; it is a song that is steeped in the Old Testament. The words are scarcely Mary's words at all; they are from the treasury of psalmist and of prophet. "My soul doth magnify the Lord"—that long ago had been the cry of Hannah. "He hath showed strength with His arm"—that is not Mary's, it is David's. And there are words of Job, in the *Magnificat*, and thoughts taken from the song of Moses, and golden utterances of Isaiah. That does not mean that Mary was a plagiarist. It does not mean that for that tumultuous hour she scanned the pages of psalmist and of prophet. It means that Mary had a heart so full of all that was written in the Word of God, that in that hour it came welling to her lips. Upon the Word she had fed her heart. She had lived in the fellowship of all its noble teaching. In maiden meditation, fancy free, she had turned to the glorious heritage of Israel. In the quiet and unrecorded years of girlhood she had prayed and studied in the light of heaven, and now the witness of the years was in her speech.

Is not that one mark of our great hours? Do they not reveal the life we have been living? Do they not show what we have loved or hated in the hidden days when there was none to see? And so in this great hour of Mary's life, when she is lifted into the gaze of all the world, the past that stands revealed to all the world is one of beautiful and earnest piety. No need to ask now where Our Lord was taught these ancient Scriptures that He loved so truly. With such a mother, whose heart and life were full of them, we can understand the secret now. That wonderful knowledge of prophet and of psalmist that was the sword of Jesus as it was His stay, began in the teaching at His mother's knee.

I close by asking you if you remember what is the last glimpse we get of Mary? It is one of the most beautiful touches in the Scriptures. It is not an appearance of the risen Christ to her, for we never read that He appeared to Mary. It is not a vision of her as the queen of heaven, for she is never mentioned in the Revelation. It is something far more womanly than that; something far more human and more tender. After Jesus had ascended into glory we read of a little company who gathered in Jerusalem—in the upper room, to pray. And that is the last glimpse we get of Mary—for the Apostle tells us *she* was there—and so in prayer she passed out of sight. Not reigning on any heavenly throne, not wielding any authority with Christ, not lifted up in any queenly dignity with the universe worshiping the Mother of God. But a woman—praying—like any other sinner, whose only hope of power and peace and glory lay in the work that ended on the Cross.

It is with that last thought we think of Mary. It is thus that she, too, leads us to the Savior. For all her wonderful ministry to Christ, we love her, and adore the hand that chose her. And then like her, in prayer, we turn to Him by Whom we live, in Whom we hope to die; Whose is the only Name given among men whereby we must be saved.

O Come, O Come, Immanuel!

James S. Stewart (1896-1990) pastored three churches in Scotland before becoming professor of theology at the University of Edinburgh (1936) and then professor of New Testament (1946). But he is a professor who can preach, a scholar who can apply biblical truth to the needs of the common man, and a theologian who can make doctrine both practical and exciting. He has published several books of lectures and biblical studies, including *A Man in Christ* and *Heralds of God*. His two finest books of sermons are *The Gates of New Life* and *The Strong Name*. This sermon is taken from *The Gates of New Life*, published in Edinburgh in 1937 by T. & T. Clark.

James S. Stewart

3

O COME, O COME, IMMANUEL!

Comfort ye, comfort ye my people, saith your God. Speak ye comfortably to Jerusalem, and cry unto her, that her warfare is accomplished, that her iniquity is pardoned (Isaiah 40:1,2)

TODAY WE ARE standing in the gateway of the Advent season; and I wish that the authentic thrill of Advent could lay some deep spell upon our spirits.

What does Advent mean? It means the glory of the coming of the Lord. It means the breaking in of the divine into human history, of the supernatural into the natural. It means a sense of something great impending from the side of heaven.

The world is blundering in a morass of sin and sorrow now, and Abyssinia goes out into the dark, and the streets of Spain run blood, and men lose hope completely; but here and there some man, some group of men, some Church stands listening and intent—for God is marching on. That is Advent.

And people have their personal problems too: and there are brave faces which hide sore hearts, and secret wounds that ache, and a restlessness new every morning; and life is terribly much harder for some than any who see them can imagine, and even God seems to have forgotten to be gracious; but sometimes through the darkness shines a light, and the troubled heart grows calm again. "Be still, my soul; for God will surely come." That is Advent.

The Wings of Music

I wish we could all recapture the authentic thrill of this dear Advent time. But words are poor things to convey it: it needs the wings of music. Some of us were listening to Sir Walford Davies' recent broadcast talk on "Melodies of Christendom." "We want to help you to catch the Advent

27

spirit," he said; and then his singers sang—sang first one
of those mighty melodies of Bach in which the passionate,
desperate yearnings of generations and centuries of men
have been caught and concentrated, sang next of the joy
when midnight turns to morning:

> "'Wake, awake! for night is flying,'
> The watchmen on the heights are crying,
> 'Awake, Jerusalem, at last!'"

I think that songs and hymns and music can carry us
nearer to the burning heart of the Advent message than
all the sermons and discourses in the world. And so I
hope that what I cannot do may be accomplished for some
in this church today when the time comes for us to sing
our final hymn, that great cry of the souls of men which
the Church for eight hundred years has lifted up to heaven:
"O come, O come, Immanuel" (you cannot sing it without
seeing a multitude of hands stretched out to God in
passionate pleading down the ages):

> "O come, O come, Immanuel,
> And ransom captive Isreal,
> That mourns in lonely exile here
> Until the Son of God appear"—

and then—the great crashing chords of triumphant
reassurance:

> "Rejoice! rejoice! Immanuel
> Shall come to thee, O Israel."

That is Advent.

The Call to Comfort

And that is the spirit of our text. "Comfort ye, comfort
ye My people, saith your God." I know, of course, that the
Advent gospel has another side to it. I know there is a day
of the Lord that is like a thief in the night. I have read the
Word of God, and heard its great commission—"Cry aloud!
Spare not! Lift up thy voice like a trumpet!" I have hear
the terrible, startling urgency that was in the voice of
Jesus when He tried to shake men awake from their

sleep, lest they should be found with loins ungirt and lamps unlit when at midnight came the cry. But I know also this, that beneath all the drums and thunder of the Advent Symphony there is a deeper undertone, the music of the peace of God that passeth understanding; "Comfort ye, comfort ye My people, saith your God."

"If I had my ministry to live through again," said a dear saint of God at the close of a long life, "I should strike the note of comfort far oftener than I have done." I think one begins to understand that. And if there were only one more sermon to preach, one last message to deliver, before the night descended, and the kindly lights of life went out, I think the text would have to be, not "Be not deceived, God is not mocked," nor anything of the kind, but rather this: "The eternal God is thy refuge, and underneath are the everlasting arms," or those dearest of the words of Jesus, "Come unto Me, all ye that labor and are heavy laden," or this of Jesus' greatest herald, "Comfort ye, comfort ye My people, saith your God."

This is not being sentimental. There is undoubtedly a type of character which accepts the consolations of religion, wallows in them in fact, without ever facing the challenge of religion. That is sentimental. That is the kind of follower who brings down the name of Jesus in the eyes of the world. "Sentimentalism is enjoyment without obligation," said George Meredith. But the true comfort of Christ is a strong, bracing, reinforcing thing. It is like a wind to a boat that has been becalmed. It is like the gift of a job to a man who has been for years out of work. It is like the clasp of a friend's hand in a time of need. This is certainly the root idea of the word "comfort" in the New Testament; and when Jesus speaks of the Holy Spirit as the "Comforter," He is really giving a promise that God will stand by a man in the day of his need, and brace his heart and nerve his arm, and make him more than conqueror. It ought surely to be possible to proclaim that without sentimentalism. I should be failing you if I attempted for one moment to minimize or to conceal the essential hardness of Christianity: it is going to be hard to the end of the day. But I should be failing you even more if I did not tell you of this comforting Christ. "Speak ye comfortably to Jerusalem," or, as the words are better translated, "Speak ye home to the heart of Jerusalem"; and "Comfort ye My people, saith your God."

Jerusalem! Think of her for a moment. How terribly she needed comfort! All that chequered history behind her—the dreams that flickered out on Mount Gilboa, where Saul and Jonathan lay dead ("Ye daughters of Israel, weep over Saul: how are the mighty fallen!"), the glory of David tarnished by the unguarded hour when Bathsheba meant more to him than God, the long battle of the prophets with recrudescent paganism when Baal renewed his hold, the thunder of Sennacherib's legions down the plains of Esdraelon and across the borders of Judah, the bitterness of the Babylonian bondage when the exiles wept for Zion and the harps hung silent on the willows ("How shall we sing the Lord's song in a strange land? If I forget thee, O Jerusalem!"), the eyes peering through the dark, the voices crying "How long, O Lord, how long?" the hands battering importunately at heaven's gate, the cry from the last ramparts of the soul, "Watchman! Watchman! Will the night soon pass?"

All that—for centuries—and then, "Comfort ye, comfort ye My people, saith your God!" And so the new dawn came.

Comfort Now

It was needed then, that note of comfort: is it not needed now? Think of God looking down at this world today, where man at war with man cannot hear the love-song of the angels, God seeing all the pathetic wreckage of broken hope with which the sea of life is littered, and man's struggles and gropings for the light—what do you imagine God must be feeling, as He contemplates the human scene? Anger? Impatience? Contempt? Disdain? Surely the writer of the old psalm knew better when, out of his own experience of what life and parenthood had taught him, he wrote the words, "Like as a father pitieth his children, so pitieth the Lord!"

You will remember a poem of Coventry Patmore's—

"The Toys," he calls it—which tells how one day his little son, having been disobedient, was sent to bed unkissed, and how the father, relenting, crept up later that night into the room, and there the child lay asleep, his face still wet with tears; and near his head on a little table he had gathered some favorite toys—a box of counters, a few shells, one or two copper coins—to comfort his sad small heart; and as the father kissed those childish tears away and left others of his own, it occurred to him that perhaps God might be feeling towards all His sons and daughters of this world just as he felt that night towards his own sleeping child:

"When Thou rememberest of what toys
We made our joys,
How weakly understood
Thy great commanded good,
Then, fatherly not less
Than I whom Thou hast molded from the clay,
Thou'lt leave Thy wrath, and say,
'I will be sorry for their childishness.'"

"Like as a father pitieth, so pitieth the Lord His children." And surely if ever that was true, it must be true about this wayward, blundering, unhappy world today; and "Comfort ye My people, saith your God."

Comfort Me

But God does not deal with men in the mass, and to talk about God comforting the world may sound remote and leave us cold. It is the individual message of Advent we want to capture. What does this deep saying in Isaiah mean for me? There are souls by the ten thousand needing comfort today. Has Advent anything for them?

I think, as one grows older, one learns to look at humanity with new eyes of wonder and of reverence: for countless are the hidden heroisms of every day. Doubtless a cynic, looking at human nature, will see only drabness and mediocrity and commonplaceness and irritating stupidity; but the man who sees only that—though he be the cleverest wit imaginable—is proclaiming himself blind and a fool. He is missing everything. He is missing the shining gallantry and fortitude which are everywhere in action. You cannot go through this world with your eyes open, and with some degree of sympathy in your soul, without realizing sooner or later that one of the crowning glories of the world—a thing that might well make the morning stars sing together and the sons of God shout for joy—is the sheer valor with which multitudes of men and women, quite unknown to fame, are carrying themselves in the face of difficulties calculated to break their hearts.

Take any gathered company of people—think of the troubled spirits that are there among them, baffled and bewildered because life has treated them unkindly, and yet keeping their heads up, and making no complaint; some worried about their health, wondering how they will be able to keep going, and what will happen to their dear ones when they finally have to give in; men out in the world, bearing the burden and heat of the day, and strained almost to the limit of their endurance by the fierce competition of this modern age; fathers and mothers anxious about children whose characters seem subtly changing, losing something of the frankness and fineness and tenderness that once was there; young people grappling with temptations which they have never been able to tell to any one; souls that have gone down defeated in the fight, despising themselves for their defeat, eager for some secret that will turn defeat to victory; lives that have had their hour of thrilling joy and springtime, and then it has vanished, and the world has grown gray and chill and wintry, and weary all life's journey now, on to the very end; conflicts which none can understand except the one who has to face them; lonelinesses that hurt; disabilities that handicap; renunciations that are a crown of thorns; memories that bless, and memories that burn, and memories that are a crucifixion. Ah, friends, look on any gathering of your fellow-men and women, try to see them, not with the eyes of cheap criticism, but with the eyes of God—and you will behold there the gold of courage, and the shining precious jewels of a chivalry like the chivalry of Christ.

Let Me Comfort Others
More than that. You will wish to God that you could be a helper and comforter. One feels so helpless often. It is like watching a loved one suffering some terrible physical pain. "O God, why cannot I suffer this instead? Lord, give it to me, and let that other off!" One feels so helpless. And one so longs to help.

Principal Denney was listening one day to a friend of his own, a missionary from the New Hebrides, telling the graphic story of how one of the New Hebridean islands had received the comfort of the gospel, and had been changed from darkness to light. And when the story was over, "I'd rather have done a work like that," said Denney, "than have written all the best books in the library."

And there are hours—I am sure they must have come to you—when you would rather have been able to comfort one dear soul in trouble than have known all the speculative philosophy in the world. "Comfort ye, comfort ye My people, saith your God."

Have you ever thought how utterly Jesus devoted Himself to this? There are commentators who tell us that Jesus did His miracles of healing to impress the onlookers and to prove His claims. I think not. He did them because He could not bear to see God's children suffering. The poor mother of Nain, crying as if her heart would break as she stumbled after the pathetic little procession going out to bury her only son—Christ could not bear it. The leper, the innocent, once happy young life struck down by that slow, dreadful living death—Christ could not bear it. "I will: be thou clean." The great mass of attractive, lovable men and women caught in the toils of sins that spoilt their lives, and temptations they could not break, and wild regrets that were a misery—Christ could not bear it. And so He died to free them. And so we can say today, in those most moving words of our hymn, "Jesus, Thou art all compassion" (I beg you, never sing these words unthinkingly, but take them home to yourself, and say, "This is true, and true for me"),

> "Jesus, Thou art all compassion,
> Pure, unbounded love Thou art;

Visit us with Thy salvation,
Enter every trembling heart."

The Compassionate Christ

But the greatest thing of all is this, that when you see this compassionate Christ, you are seeing God. This is the comfort which the Advent tidings bring—and it is all in that one word Immanuel: for Immanuel means "God with us," with us in Jesus, God going through the darkness with you, God saying, "My friend, you must not carry the trouble alone any longer—cast it down at My feet: I will take it and carry it, and the hardest part shall be My part!" The word Immanuel means that where we, with all our poor human words of comfort, break down utterly, God begins. Immanuel means that when you feel nobody wants you, God does. Immanuel means that when your heart is crying to every would-be comforter, "Ah, you don't understand, you can't see things from my side of them, you are outside"—Immanuel means that God is right inside. Immanuel means God with you and in you, God making the pain a sacrament, the conflict a crusade, and the broken dreams a ladder up to heaven. And so, through Christ, God speaks home to the heart of Jerusalem.

But you know and I know that there is one comfort we need more than any other, more than the soothing of our sorrows and the calming of our cares; and that is, the forgiving of our sins. There is no real comfort until the conscience is at peace, and the heart is clean, and the will is right with God. But the glory of this great word Immanuel is that it means even that. For listen to what stands written. It is not only "Speak to the heart of Jerusalem," but "Cry unto her that her iniquity is pardoned!" And it is "Cry to her" this time, not "Speak quietly to her heart," but "Cry it aloud!"—as much as to say, "She will not believe it at first. She will not want to accept it. It will sound too good to be true. You will have to make these tidings urgent. Cry to her that all is forgiven!"

It is on this level that God's greatest work is done. I began by saying that I wished I could help you to capture the authentic thrill of Advent. I end now by saying that this is it—nothing less—that it is on those battlefields where men and women struggle for their souls we have sometimes met defeat; if things have happened and have left a mark, and we know they ought never to have been; if the shades of the prison-house of habit have come closing in around us; if we have tasted shame, and self-despising, and have lost the morning freshness of our souls; if, like those Jews in Babylon, we have felt ourselves exiled from the face of God—then this is the thrill of Advent, to hear the great Father saying, "My son, My daughter, that is all past now, and done with and finished forever," to find every barrier broken down by the love of Christ and the old dear intimacy restored, to know that you can enter, this very moment, into a new world of light and joy and liberty. We are going to sing of it now, in the greatest of Advent songs. God grant the experience of it to us all!

> "O come, Thou Key of David, come,
> And open wide our heavenly home;
> Make safe the way that leads on high,
> And close the path to misery.
> Rejoice! rejoice! Immanuel
> Shall come to thee, O Israel."

Peace Among Men of God's Pleasure

George Campbell Morgan (1863-1945) was the son of a British Baptist preacher, and he preached his first sermon when he was 13 years old. He had no formal training for the ministry, but his tireless devotion to the study of the Bible helped him to become one of the leading Bible teachers of his day. Rejected by the Methodists, he was ordained into the Congregational ministry. He was associated with Dwight L. Moody in the Northfield Bible conferences and as an itinerant Bible teacher. He is best known as the pastor of the Westminster Chapel, London (1904-17 and 1933-45). During his second term there, he had Dr. D. Martyn Lloyd-Jones as his associate. Morgan published more than 60 books and booklets, and his sermons are found in *The Westminster Pulpit* (London, Pickering and Inglis, 1906-16). This sermon is from Volume 6.

George Campbell Morgan

4

PEACE AMONG MEN OF GOD'S PLEASURE

Glory to God in the highest, And on earth peace among men in whom He is well pleased (Luke 2:14).

THESE WORDS CONSTITUTED the angelic anthem of welcome to the New Race. The angel messenger had told the shepherds of "a babe wrapped in swaddling clothes, and lying in a manger." In this chorus the angels expressed their understanding of the significance of the event, "Glory to God in the highest." The term "in the highest" does not signify degree but location; "the highest" in the text stands in contrast to the earth, not necessarily separated from it, but suggesting the fact of the two spheres, earth and heaven.

> Glory to God in the *highest,*
> And *on earth* peace among men in whom
> He is well pleased.

This was more than the song that celebrated the birth of the Babe; it was the song that celebrated the race which was to result from the birth of the Babe. The terms are quite explicit: peace, not toward men, but among men. However much we may differ about the translation and interpretation of that which remains of the passage, about this there is no doubt, that it is not peace or good will *toward* men, but *among* men—peace among men in whom He is well pleased. That is at once the limitation of the thought and the indication of the true region of peace.

The significance of the song which the angels sang will be discovered in recognition of the Biblical teaching concerning the interest which angels have taken in this world of ours. Their first song about the world, according to Biblical revelation, is recorded in the book of Job, in that wonderful passage of the Theophany or unveiling of God before the astonished vision of His servant, tried, buffeted and bruised by temptation. In the course of that great unveiling it is declared that when God laid the cornerstone of the earth,

> The Morning stars sang together
> And all the sons of God shouted for joy.

You will remember that Milton couples these songs—the song of creation and the song of the Advent of the Savior—in the great hymn of the Nativity, when he sings:

> Such music (as 'tis said),
> Before was never made.
>   But when of old the sons of morning sang
> While the Creator great
> His constellations set,
>   And the well-balanced word on hinges hung
> And cast the dark foundations deep
> And bid the welt'ring waves their oozy channel keep.

Such is the first Scripture suggestion about angel interest. They sang in creation.

If Faber was right when he sang that

> There is no place where earth's sorrows
> Are more felt than up in heaven,

then angel sons had surely merged from the major shoutings of creation's dawn into minor wailings in view of the miseries of men resulting from their sin. I immediately say to you that I think Faber was quite right, that there is no place where earth's sorrows are more felt than up in heaven. All sorrow there is transfigured by the light that we know not yet; all sorrow there is modified, and experienced within its relationship to the infinite movements; but sorrow is surely there, for it is in the heart of God Himself in the presence of human suffering and misery. I repeat, I verily believe that often the angels had sung in minor wailing over the miseries of men.

Now at last, as the angel said to the shepherds, "there is born . . . in the city of David a Savior, which is Christ the Lord." To those angel singers the One born was "a second man," "the last Adam." In the view of the angels His birth was a new commencement in human history. From that child lying in the manger they saw a new race springing, and in celebration of the new race they raised their anthem:

> Glory to God in the highest,
> And on earth peace among men in whom
> He is well pleased.

The first note of the anthem was a recognition of the Source of the New Movement, "Glory to God in the highest." The central note celebrated the issue which had happened that day, "on earth peace." The final note revealed the condition of realization, "among men in whom He is well pleased."

If thus, in this anthem, we discover the note of limitations, and surely it is here, let us remember that the limitation is but declared in order to reveal the condition on which the ultimate purpose may be realized. There can be no question that at last the men of His good pleasure, the men in whom He is well pleased, will be men of all kindreds and races, that, at last, "though a wide compass first be fetched," His victory is secure; that, although the process may be one of conflict and long and painful struggle in the history of the world, yet finally the note of the angel anthem will be found to be the chord of the dominant, and all the music of human conditions will be true to its suggestion.

Let us briefly consider these three things in a slightly different order: first, the issue described, "on earth peace"; second, the condition revealed, "among men in whom He is well pleased"; and, finally, in a closing and brief word, the source suggested, "Glory to God in the highest."

The Issue Described

First, then, "on earth peace." Is it not difficult to understand that word? Probably not, in our own hearts and personal experiences as Christian men and women; for already all such as have reposed their trust in this

Lord Christ know something of that peace of God which passeth all understanding. But if we look away from these personal experiences, and endeavor to enter into the consciousness of our own times and of the conditions in the midst of which we live, is it not almost impossible to understand this phrase, "on earth peace"? That is to say, the ideal seems far from realization. If we contrast all that is suggested by this phrase with all that we find in history, how startling is the difference between peace and the perpetual conflict and unrest, the pain and suffering of the world. I do not desire to dwell particularly on matters that are wholly immediate and local, and yet we are all painfully conscious of the actual condition of the world. We are all conscious, for instance, of the fact that the world's national peace is a mockery and a sham, that it is merely an armed neutrality based on suspicion. We are all terribly, and more acutely, conscious of the fact that the very peace of our own life is often rudely broken in on by the shock of strife and catastrophe. Where is peace?

Without staying to deal with other evidences of immediate unrest, let us take a broader outlook, and I think a deeper inlook, and inquire what are the underlying reasons as there shall come to men who are conscious of moral malady. Peace can come only to men who are conscious of suffering without succor or sympathy that is more than sentiment, as there comes to them the succor that takes hold of suffering and transmutes the sorrow into joy, and gives them the assurance that not here and now is all of that which is here and now, but that the ultimate meanings lie beyond. In the economy of God they are meanings of perfect realization. Peace can come only to a world where death confronts men, when, somehow, death can be transfigured, and men cease to speak of death, and talk instead of decease, of exodus, going out. Peace can come only when death is no longer looked on as a harbor of refuge into which the ship all battered escapes, but rather as the harbor from which the ship puts out to sea and finds the ultimate fulfillment of all being. These are Christian ideals, and can be realized by men only when they enter into Christian experience.

The Condition Revealed

We now turn to that which is central to this meditation, the suggestion of the angels concerning the condition of peace, "peace among men in whom He is well pleased." This song was sung, first, because of the birth of the Babe. I take up this gospel portraying the perfection of Jesus of Nazareth, and I trace the story through a little way in order that we may catch the fuller meaning of the angel song, "Glory to God in the highest, and on earth peace among men in whom He is well pleased."

I turn to the fortieth verse of the first chapter, and I read:

> And the child grew, and waxed strong, filled with wisdom: and the grace of God was upon him.

That was twelve years afterwards, measuring the life by human measurements.

I run on down the same chapter to the fifty-second verse; eighteen more years have passed, thirty years from the hour of the angel song, and now I read:

> Jesus advanced in wisdom and stature, and in favor with God and man.

I go a little further in this wonderful story of His life and I read in the third chapter, verse twenty-two:

> A voice came out of heaven, Thou art My beloved Son; in Thee I am well pleased.

Why, then, was the song sung? Because there in the manger lying was the Babe in Whom God was well pleased. This does not suggest that God is not well pleased in the presence of every child, every babe, but it does suggest a difference. It suggests this initial fact of absolute perfection, a new beginning in human history, a strange wonder never to be finally understood. There was the Child, the first of a new race. There is a sense today in which any child that lies in its mother's arms, every little one, is dear to His heart, dearer than to the mother who nurses it. But there were peculiar facts about this Child. As a Boy the grace of God was on Him; as a Man of thirty it is declared that He had grown in favor with God and man.

Then Luke tells us that the heavens were opened and a voice declared, "Here is the Man in Whom I am well pleased." In Him, then, there is peace, for peace is among men in whom He is well pleased.

And still further we follow the story as Luke tells it, and in the first and second verses of the fourth chapter we read:

> And Jesus, full of the Holy Spirit, returned from the Jordan, and was led by the Spirit in the wilderness during forty days, being tempted of the devil.

There He mastered all temptations.

Still reading on in order to discover the music that follows the angelic anthem, we find in the fourteenth verse of the same chapter:

> And Jesus returned in the power of the Spirit.

He went to service and to sacrifice, until, let it be reverently stated, "He offered Himself through the eternal Spirit." All the way from the beginning to the end we see the Man in Whom God is well pleased.

Thus we see peace, focused in one human being, peace in the Man in whom God was well pleased. He was a lowly Man, at first a Babe, then a Boy, then a Man, and through all a Servant. One Who went to death in the fulfillment of His service; and all the way He was a Man of peace.

Now, do not let us be anxious for the moment about the ultimate application of all this, but let us earnestly behold this Man of Nazareth, the Man of peace. If there is one thing more certain than anything else in the revelation of Jesus in these gospels it is that of His peace. In neither of these gospel stories can we find any occasion, any circumstance, any hour, in which He was perturbed. Always He is the Man of peace.

When we come to the final scenes—and I cannot tell you why it is so, but I never come to Christmas now without feeling that the cradle and the Cross are close together—I cannot think of Him Who came and rejoice in His coming without thinking of the ultimate in the mystery of His passion; I say, when we come to those last tragic scenes, we find that the One human being, undisturbed, quiet, and strong, was the Man of peace, not the priests, who were determined to ensure His murder, not the cool, dispassionate Roman Procurator Pilate, who was strangely perturbed; but Jesus only was quiet and at peace.

What was this experience of His peace? A perfect and perpetual victory over sin, the constant transmutation of suffering in His own life, so that under the very shadow of the Cross in the midst of those paschal discourses He could say to His disciples, "My joy"; and, speaking of the deepest thing in His life, the annihilation of death, long before He was apprehended and crucified, He had said, "I lay down My life, that I may take it again, No one taketh it away from Me, but I lay it down of Myself." Even on the holy mount, having come to the fulfillment of His humanity in the splendor of the metamorphosis, He spoke, not of the death He should die, but of the exodus He should accomplish. In these three things I find the secrets of His peace.

But is that all the angels meant? Nay verily! They sang not only of the Babe, but also of the race that was to spring from Him; not merely of peace in the Man of His good pleasure, but of "peace among men in whom He is well pleased."

Now let us run from Luke to John, and in that gospel so brief in many respects, and yet so full of understanding of the deepest things in the life and ministry of our Lord, we find that in the midst of the paschal discourses, with the shadow of the Cross upon Him, and the last things close at hand, talking to a little group of men, He said:

"Peace I leave with you; My peace I give unto you: not as the world giveth give I unto you. Let not your heart be troubled, neither let it be fearful" (John 14:27).

And for these men that was the day when they were more troubled and afraid than they had ever been in their lives; it was the day when all the restlessness of the world seemed to be their portion, the day when hope was dying down and every gleam of light seemed wholly vanishing, the day when high and holy aspirations seemed doomed to utter disappointment in that He persisted in going out to die! Yet on that day He said, "Peace I leave with you; My peace I give unto you."

Then follow the next pages in the gospel of John, telling the story of dark days for them, days in which there came the end of all peace; the moral malady against which He had protested was victorious over Him, and He was murdered, suffering without succor finding its final expression in His untold sorrow, as they watched Him as long as they were able and then fled for very fear; death, which He had seemed to count as a small matter in the whole economy of life mastered Him, and He was put into the grave; and all that after He had said, "Peace I leave with you." I am in sympathy with these men in their sorrow and in their inevitable sense that peace was no more.

Now let us turn to the twentieth chapter. Here we find ourselves in the midst of a little company of terrified souls gathered in an upper room with doors locked. I have no criticism for them. I would have shared their fear. I think I would have been more fearful than they, and hardly been present at all. Suddenly standing in the midst is the same One, the Man of God's good pleasure. What is the first word that passes His lips? "Peace be unto you." It was His answer to their fear. And again in a few moments, "Peace be unto you." It was His preparation for their service. Eight days later, with Thomas the great believer present, again He said, "Peace be unto you." It was the call to faith.

From that moment the number of men of peace in the world was multiplied. Much later John wrote, "As He is, even so are we in this world." Was there ever such a daring word written under inspiration? Yet in this very matter of peace how true it was! The peacefulness of Christ's witnesses under persecution has been one of the world's perpetual wonders.

What created the peace that possessed these men and sent them out in the midst of the world's suffering and conflict and darkness? They shared His peace. What was His peace? Victory over sin. The transmutation of suffering, so that these men—mark the true and deep mystery of the word in Acts—are seen "rejoicing that they were counted worthy to suffer dishonor for the Name." Finally, the annihilation of death, for when they write their letters these men will not speak of death as other men speak of death; they will take up His words and use them, and Peter will say, After my *exodus*, using the very word that Jesus used on the holy mount; and Paul will say, After my *departure*, that is my going away out into the larger life. These are the secrets of peace, "peace among men in whom He is well pleased."

The Source Suggested

In a final word, notice the suggestion of the angels concerning the source, "Glory to God in the highest." Salvation must come from God and not from man. Salvation must come out of the heavens to the earth; it cannot arise out of the earth and climb to the heavens. Therefore, glory to God is a necessity as it is a fact.

When the Babe was born a movement began that will issue in a race in which He is well pleased. That was the meaning of Christmas to the angels. Who is this Child? He is the Son of God, the Lord from heaven. He is also the Babe of the new race, Who, not by human will or act, laid hold on humanity and entered thereinto for a new beginning, for the accomplishment of the larger purposes of God. Those angels, then, sang o'er the plains of Bethlehem not of the Babe alone, but of the race.

Take this Christ away and all the conditions of unrest abide: moral malady without remedy, suffering without succor and with no proof of God's sympathy, and death as an appalling darkness out of which no ray of certain light shines and out of which no voice comes, and we still shall have to describe it as "the borne whence no traveler returns." Take this Christ-child away, then, and peace is impossible.

But the Christ-child is not taken away. We are not merely celebrating a far-off event, we are gathered around the presence of the living Lord Himself, and around all the great eternal facts focused, and rendered visible, by the mystery of Incarnation and by way of the Cross.

Consequently, if our trust is reposed in Him we are people of peace, we are people in whom God by grace is well pleased. Already in us He finds the forces of His own life and of the Son of His love; and He knows that the deepest facts of our lives are those, and that at last they will bring a perfect and final salvation and an eternal peace. Thus while yet we are in the midst of the clash of battle there is peace.

If you take this Christ away, have you any song to sing worth the singing? I know full well that tragedy sometimes makes faith falter. I know what it is—and if there are those who do not, then let them be patient with me, for I speak not for myself alone—I know what it is in some hour of calamity to say, Where is God? But my question does not alter the calamity; and if I am allowing my unbelief to silence these angels, to hush these bells, to deny this music, then, God help me, what is life?

Oh, hear the song of the angels over all sighing humanity. We are celebrating today the infinite mystery, and mystery it is, of incarnate God. From it all light is streaming, and all songs are coming, all hope is flaming, and we believe that at last there shall be peace.

> Joy to the world! the Lord is come;
> Let earth receive her King;
> Let every heart prepare Him room,
> And heaven and nature sing.

NOTES

The Christ of Christmas

Walter A. Maier (1893-1950) was known around the world as the speaker on "The Lutheran Hour," heard over more than a thousand radio stations. Many of his faithful listeners did not realize that this effective communicator was also a professor of Old Testament and Semitic Languages at Concordia Seminary in St. Louis. It was said that Maier spent one hour in preparation for each minute that he spoke on the air. Numbers of his radio sermons were published in volumes still treasured by those who appreciate good preaching. This sermon is found in *The Lutheran Hour*, published by Concordia Publishing House, St. Louis, in 1931.

Walter A. Maier

5

THE CHRIST OF CHRISTMAS

Unto us a Child is born, unto us a Son is given: and the government shall be upon His shoulder. And His name shall be called Wonderful, Counselor. The Mighty God, The Everlasting Father, The Prince of Peace (Isaiah 9:6).

ONLY FIVE HOURS more in the Pacific Coast country, only two short hours on the Atlantic seaboard, and another Christmas will be but a memory. A few moments more to linger in the colorful radiance of the Christmas-tree, a few moments more to blend our hearts and voices in the cheerful Christmas melodies, a few moments more to enjoy the happiness that comes to our reunited family circles on Christmas, and this day of days from which we unwillingly release our grasp is gone and has given way to the tomorrow, in which, as men resume their wonted activities, the spell of Christmas is often broken, its luster dimmed, its message forgotten.

But Christmas is too wonderfully magnificent to be confined to one solitary, fleeting day. There is rather a deathless significance in this Child of Christmas, a permanent and divinely bestowed gift of God, which brings perpetual happiness, immeasurable and unspeakable, both here and hereafter. And if you have never permitted the star of faith to guide you to Bethlehem; if you have never opened the door of your heart to receive the Christ-child; if with Herodlike determination you have steadfastly tried to stifle the glorification of the Babe in Bethlehem, to what better advantage can I employ these happy moments than to ask you to separate your hearts from all earth-born attachments, to submerge the harsh dissonance of cold doubt and frigid skepticism, to follow the lowly shepherds to that glorious Child in Mary's arms, and to immortalize Christmas as a hope of perpetual and undying happiness by hearing and believing the divine and

49

unfailing answer to this question, Who is this Child about whom the very universe revolves, in whom the hopes and fears of all the years have found their joyous fulfillment?

Seven centuries before the heavenly messenger aroused the drowsy Judean shepherds, Isaiah, the evangelist of the Old Testament, straining his gaze to the dim and distant horizon, answered this question in better terms than merely mortal lips can find. Casting aside the modern *camouflage*, which finds in the birth of Jesus Christ only such alien thoughts as the magnificence of motherhood or the glorification of childhood, and probing deep down beneath the externals of our Christmas celebration, he strikes at the very heart and center of a Christ-conscious Christmas, when, in those deathless words beginning, *"Unto us a Child is born, unto us a Son is given,"* he identifies this Christmas-child by these five glorious names, *"Wonderful, Counselor, The Mighty God, The Everlasting Father, The Prince of Peace,"* and tells us tonight who this Christ-child is and what He must mean to our modern world after nineteen centuries.

"Wonderful"

Isaiah calls the Christ-child, first of all, *"Wonderful,"* or, as we can emphatically reproduce the original, "The Miracle." Daniel Webster was once asked whether he could understand Christ. Replying in the negative, he declared that, if he could understand Him, there would be nothing to give Jesus faith and divine force and fact. The Christmas-message is thus not an appeal to reason, to be sure; and we breathe an ardent word of thankful prayer that it is something ineffably greater than this. It is an appeal to the truth of God's love; it is the mystery of God's becoming man; Divinity putting on humanity; the Creator appearing as creature; the eternal Son of God incarnate as the Son of Man. In an age when men glibly and confidently prate about the twilight of Christianity, as they compose their obituaries on the Biblical truth, the cold and calculating rationalizing of reason bids them ask with age-old skepticism, "How can these things be? How can this Child, called the *'Wonderful,'* be both divine and human, both a helpless babe and the Ruler of the universe," of whom our text says, *"The government shall be upon His shoulder,"* implying that He directs the affairs of men, controls the forces of nature, and governs this vast universe? But as the first Christmas-gifts were expressive of the willing tribute which scientific thought paid to religious verities, so today, when we daily accept uncounted arrangements and innumerable procedures as beyond the ken of the most enlightened mind, let no one who hears the Christmas evangel indulge in skeptical quibbles or sophisticated sneers, but let us rather rejoice that instead of understanding we must only believe and kneel down before this Wonder of the Ages to offer, as Magi-minded Christians, the pure gold of our faith, the fragrant frankincense of our hope, and mystic myrrh of our love.

But the wonder of this Child, the supreme miracle in the history of all lands and ages, becomes intensified when we realize, as I pray God we may all realize on this joyful Christmas Day, that this Babe in the manger is the superhuman solution to the great and universal problem of sin. When the stern demand of God's holiness tells you, *"The soul that sinneth, it shall die";* when it continues its warning indictment, *"All have sinned";* and when it individually emphasizes the weaknesses and inconsistencies that abound in every life and says, as it points the finger of accusation at you, *"Thou art the man"*— then to every one who humbly and gratefully accepts Christmas for what its name implies, the wonder of wonders is accomplished, and they all are assured of this miracle-working love, announced even before the Child's birth, *"He shall save His people from their sins."* There is the glorious wonder of this wonderful Child—no sin too great, no offense too vile, no wrong too oppressive to be removed freely and completely and for all time by His priceless, deathless love.

"The Counselor"

The second blessed name of the Christ of Christmas is *"The Counselor."* I believe that for many thousands who are listening in tonight the need of a capable, competent counselor has perhaps never been as great as it is on this Christmas Day, when we remind ourselves that the past year has brought to millions a long series of disappointments of various kinds and degrees. You who have gone on year after year with a smug sense of self-satisfaction and with a good deal of confidence in your money power, your brain power, your social power, but who have found that this house of cards in which you have enshrined your happiness has been puffed over by bank failures, financial reverses, war, and unemployment, and who now look about for some one and something that can effectively lift you out of the labyrinth of hopelessness and helplessness—you can find a divine *Counselor* today in Bethlehem. Here is a *Counselor* who is concerned first and foremost about the soul that lives on after the trinkets and baubles that men clutch so frantically crumble into disappointing dust. Here is the faithful and efficient *Counselor*, who tells us, *"Seek ye first the kingdom of God"*; that is, get right with God. Remove the barrier that separates you from God and that keeps you away from the inner happiness which alone makes life worth living.

And when you come and ask, "How can I get right with God? How can I remove the impurity of sin from my life?"—great and wonderful *Counselor* that He is, this Christ tells us, *"I am the Way, the Truth, and the Life." "Believe in Me."* Never has His counsel failed; never is there any problem too intricate for His constructive solution; never is there any sorrow too deep to be healed by the balm of His consoling love. So tonight, when the joy of Christmas stands out in crying contrast to the sorrow that reigns in the hearts of some of my audience, when you think of your own misfortunes, of the gladness that has been turned to sadness through the coming of cold death or through the blasting of long-cherished hopes or through the tragedy that has followed in the wake of grievous sins; look above these difficulties to the *Counselor*, reposed in Behtlehem's manger, and believe Him, when He calls out to you, *"Come unto Me, all ye that labor and are heavy laden, and I will give you rest."*

"The Mighty God"
The third name of this Wonder-Child is *"The Mighty God."* Here, then, we have the real, essential Christ of Christmas; not the Christ whom the barrage of modern oratory and rhetoric likes to picture—a ghastly counterfeit from the lowly beginning at Bethlehem until the bitter, heart-breaking end at Calvary claimed to be, proved to be, and was declared by God to be, God manifest in the flesh. Oh, He had to be God to offer substitution for the overpowering weight of sin and its consequences. He had to be God to give to humanity a hope that was stronger than human power, truer than mortal truth, more hopeful than earth's strongest hope.

I sometimes wonder whether beneath all the hurry and the scurry of Christmas we realize, even as far as this is humanly possible, the practical meaning of this sublime truth, that God became man, that He lived and walked and had His being here on earth, in the closest contact with sin-stained men. What unutterable love, what indescribable mercy, what unfathomable grace! And what surpassing promise! For does not He who once trod the paths of men give to those who know Him and who love Him and who have been reconciled by His atoning blood the assurance even in today's turmoil, *"Lo, I am with you alway, even unto the end of the world"?* Think of this priceless Christmas-gift of God's grace, Immanuel, *"God with us."* God with us to turn the night of sin and sorrow into the brilliancy of a radiant day! God with us to lead us on through the devious and difficult paths of life! God with us in the happiness of our homes, in the stern realities of the battle for existence! God with us in the trials and temptations that bear down upon us! God with us as the all-sufficient, all-embracing Friend, Guide, and Savior, now and forevermore!

"The Everlasting Father"
Yes, "forevermore," because Isaiah's fourth name for this helpless Infant is *"The Everlasting Father."* Paradox though they seem when applied to this Babe of Bethlehem, let us linger for a moment on these two names of majestic

import, *"Everlasting"* and *"Father."* Throughout their long and varied existence men have yearned and strained for something firm and unchangeable, for something positive and everlasting, since the highest achievements of human ambitions rise only to fade and wax only to wane. They are here today and gone tomorrow. Even the choicest products of man's intellectual attainments are ephemeral, hailed in this hour and rejected in the next. But tonight I want you to look with me at this Pillar of the Ages, this changeless Christ for a changing world—Him who is *"the same yesterday, today, and forever,"* and find in Him the everlasting Rock of Ages to which, amid the ebb and flow of man's fluctuating hopes and delusions, you can cling with unending and undying assurance. Friends and their favors may change; your hopes and plans may be shattered and crushed, but here in this Child is God's answer to your search for eternity, the solution of the mystery of the grave, the promise of Him who says, *"Because I live, ye shall live also,"* whose eternity is the unfailing pledge of our life after death.

Think of the other word, *"Father,"* and remember that behind all the love that this word expresses and the confidence that it inspires, leading us to come to Christ as loving children come to their loving father, there is the majesty of power, the mystery of the Holy Trinity, the very revelation of God to mankind. When Christ complied with Philip's request, *"Lord, show us the Father,"* He answered, *"He that hath seen me hath seen the Father."* My friends, I pause to ask you on this Christmas Day, Have you seen the Father in Christ? Remember, if you think you have seen God in any other way; if you think you can accept God without accepting Jesus Christ; if you try to stifle the appeal of the Bible by asserting that you believe in a "Supreme Being" or in "the great Creator" or in "the Father of us all," and exclude the Christ from all this, then you do not know the meaning of Christmas, and you do not know God.

"The Prince of Peace"

But the sweetest note of the Christmas-message comes in Isaiah's last name for the Christ-child, *"The Prince of*

Peace." Above all the hatred of a war-torn world the Christmas anthem *"Peace on earth"* goes out into the world tonight to tell men that the only way to establish peace with our God and peace with our conscience is to come to Christ and to believe that He has effectually and forever removed the discord that exists between the holiness of God and the unholiness of men; that He by His incarnation, by the poverty and suffering to which He as the Lord of lords and the King of kings subjected Himself, satisfied the claims of divine justice and offers to all the benefits of that momentous peace treaty between heaven and earth that has been signed and sealed by His very blood.

What more wonderful privilege could there be on the birthday of this *Prince of Peace* than to offer in His name, by His command, and with His promise the surpassing gift of this inner, spiritual peace of God? And what greater cause of rejoicing, even in heaven, than this, that some of you within the reach of my voice this evening who are still at war with God, who are still allied with the forces of sin and hell, come to accept peace—not the peace of the world, but the peace of the soul that Christ Himself, our Shiloh, offers, the peace which, because it transforms our inner life, is reechoed in our outer existence. I appeal to you who have never learned the marvelous joy of life that comes when the benediction of Christ's peace is pronounced upon your sin-free soul; to you who do not know this peace because you do not show it; to you who, although you may to all appearances kneel at the manger this night, nevertheless harbor thoughts of hatred and envy against your fellow-men; to you young people who live in strife and discord with your own fathers and mothers; to you husbands and wives who are permitting the rancor of selfishness and dissatisfaction to mar the beauty of a happy Christian home; to you who professionally promote misunderstanding and bigotry in the lives of men—I appeal to you and beseech you in the name of the Lord Jesus: Do not let this night draw to its completion without coming to the Christ-child in spirit and in truth, without asking Him for the forgiveness of these sore and besetting evils, and without receiving from Him this priceless, peerless peace of soul and mind. Thus, and thus alone, can Christmas be to you what it should be and what, pray God, it will be—the birthday of Christ, The *Prince of Peace*, not only in Bethlehem, but also in your innermost heart. Amen.

NOTES

No Room for Jesus

Dwight Lyman Moody (1837-1899) is known around the world as one of America's most effective evangelists. Converted as a teenager through the witness of his Sunday school teacher, Moody became active in YMCA and Sunday school work in Chicago while pursuing a successful business career. He then devoted his life to evangelism and was used mightily of God in campaigns in both the United States and Great Britain. He founded the Northfield School for Girls, the Mount Hermon School for Boys, the Northfield Bible Conference, and the Moody Bible Institute in Chicago. Before the days of planes and radio, Moody traveled more than a million miles and addressed more than 100 million people.

This message is from the *Great Pulpit Masters* series reprinted in 1972 by Baker Book House.

Dwight Lyman Moody

6

NO ROOM FOR JESUS

And laid him in a manger, because there was no room for them in the inn (Luke 2:7).

YOU WILL FIND my text this evening in the second chapter of the Gospel of Luke, a part of the seventh verse: "And laid him in a manger, because there was no room for them in the inn." For four thousand years the world had been looking for Christ. Prophets had been prophesying, and the mothers of Israel had been praying and hoping that they might be the mother of that child; and now He has arrived, we find that He is laid in a borrowed cradle.

"There was no room for them in the inn." He might have come with all the grandeur and glory of the upper world. He might have been ushered into this world with ten thousand angels; yea, legions upon legions of angels might have come to herald His advent. He might have been born in a palace or a castle. He might have been born upon a throne, if He had chosen to; but He just became poor, for your sake and mine. He passed by mansions and thrones and dominions, and went down into a manger.

The Borrowed Cradle

His cradle was not only borrowed, but almost everything that He had was borrowed. It was a borrowed beast He road into Jerusalem on; it was a borrowed grave they laid Him in. When the Prince of Wales came to this country, what a welcome he received. There wasn't anything too good for him. When the Prince of Russia came to this country, I saw him as he was escorted up Broadway; and cheer upon cheer went up all the way. New York felt honored that they had such a guest.

The Prince of Wales during the past few months has

been in India, and what a reception he received there! Even those heathen are glad to do him honor. When the Prince of heaven came down, what kind of a reception did He meet with? There were no hallelujahs from the people. He found that there was no room in Bethlehem for Him; there was no room in Jerusalem for Him. When he arrived at Jerusalem not only the king, but all Jerusalem was troubled. When the wise men told Herod: "He is King of the Jews, for we have seen his star in the east," not only the king upon the throne, but all Jerusalem was in trouble; and every man that had been looking for Him seemed to be troubled, and the whole city is excited. The king sends out and commands all infants under a certain age to be slain. No sooner the news comes that He is born than the sword is unsheathed, and follows Him, you may say, to Calvary.

And has the world grown better? Is not this world about like that little town in Bethlehem? There is no room for Him. What nation wants Him today? Does this nation want Him? Suppose you should put it to a popular vote, I don't believe there is a town in the whole republic that would vote for Him. Does England want Him? England and the United States are perhaps the most Christianized countries on the globe; but I don't believe there is a town in England or in this country that would vote for Him. In fact, I may say, does the Church of God want Him? We have the forms; we are satisfied with them; but we deny the power. I am ashamed to say that there are many of our churches that really would not want Him.

If Christ Came Today

There would be a different state of things in the Church of God today if Christ should come. A great many church members do not want Him; they say: "My life is not right." There are very few families in the whole city of New York that would make room for Him. They would make room for the greatest drunkard in New York rather than make room for Him. Don't think the world is better if it won't make room for Him. If He should go to Washington, do you think they would make room for Him there? If a man should get up in Congress and say, "Thus saith the Lord," they would hoot him out. If Christ should go there, they would say: "He is too good; He is too honest; we don't want Him; we don't want honest men."

When it comes to a real, personal God, the world doesn't want Him; the nations of the earth don't want Him. Does France want Him? Does Italy want Him? Oh, my friends, there is no room for Christ, yet it would be a glorious day if there was room for Him. I believe the millennium would soon be here.

When He went to Decapolis, He found a man there filled with devils, and He cast out those devils; and the people of Decapolis came out and besought Him to go out of their coasts. Take what you call the fashionable society of New York, is He wanted there? They will talk about this church and that church; they will talk about Dr. So-and-so, and the Rev. So-and-so, and talk about the Bible in schools; but when it comes to a real, personal Christ, and you ask them, "Do you want Christ in your heart?" they say, "O sir, that is out of taste." I pity the man or woman who talks in that way. Is He wanted in commerce? Is He wanted on the Stock Exchange? If He was, men would have to keep their books different. Commercial men don't want Him.

The Loneliness of Jesus

You may ask the question: "Well, where is He wanted; who wants Him? Where is there room for the Son of God? Who will make room for Him?" I wonder if there is anyone here who ever had that feeling for five minutes. I think I have had that feeling for a day. There are some who wonder how people can commit suicide. It's no wonder to me. When men feel that there is no room for them, that no one wants them; when they feel that they are a burden to their friends, and a burden to themselves, why, it drives them mad. I remember one day when I felt as if no one wanted me. I felt as if there was no room for me. For about twenty-four hours I had that awful feeling that no one wanted me. It seems to me as if that must have been the feeling of Christ. His neighbors didn't want Him; those

Nazarenes didn't want Him; they would have taken Him to the brow of the hill and dashed Him to the bottom; they would have torn Him limb from limb if they could. He went down into Capernaum; they didn't want Him there. Jerusalem didn't want Him; there was no room.

To me, there is one of the most touching verses in the Bible, in the closing part of the seventh chapter of John. I believe it is the only place where Christ was left alone: "Every man went to his own house, and Jesus went to the Mount of Olives." I have often thought I would like to have met Him upon that mount. He was on the mount alone. There was no home for Him in Jerusalem. He was looked upon as a blasphemer; some thought He was possessed of devils; and so He was left alone. You could have seen Him under an olive tree, alone, and I imagine that night you could have heard Him crying to God for His own. And perhaps it was on that memorable occasion, or a similar occasion, when He said, "The foxes have holes, and the birds of the air have nests; but the Son of man hath no where to lay his head." Thanks be to God, there was a place.

The Little Home at Bethany

I have often thought of that little home at Bethany. It says that Martha received Him into her home. It was the best thing that Martha ever did; and do you think she ever regretted it? Little did she know that her loved brother was soon going to die, when she made room for Jesus. Ah, it was the best thing that Martha and Mary ever did when they received the village carpenter, the despised Nazarene, into their home. He used to have a walk down from the city two miles to Bethany; but there He always found room.

But look again, look in that home where Lazarus comes home sick. Some think his occupation was that of a scribe, that he was a writer, and one day he came home weary; perhaps he had a headache, and fever seized him. One of the leading physicians of Jerusalem is sent for, and the third or fourth day he tells the sisters: "There is no hope for your brother, he is dying, he cannot live." And when all earthly hope had failed, and they had given up, then the sisters sent for Jesus. Those two sisters sent a messenger, perhaps one of the neighbors, off from Bethany; perhaps he would have to go twenty or thirty miles away, on the other side of Jordan, for they heard Jesus was there. They did not have papers in those days to tell them where He was, and if there had been papers in those days to tell them where He was, they wouldn't have reported His meetings. There wouldn't have been a paper that would have taken the pains to report His meetings. They instructed the messenger to say, "Him whom thou lovest is sick."

That was enough. What a title to have to a man's name! What a eulogy to have to a name! And when the messenger came and told the message, he told Him that he whom He loved was very sick; and the Lord Jesus turned to him and said, "I will go. Take back word to those two sisters. The sickness is not unto death, but I will come." And I can see those two sisters. How eager they are to find out what his success had been. "What did He say?" and the messenger answers, "Why He said the sickness was not unto death; and He would come and see Lazarus." I can imagine Mary turns to the messenger and says, "I don't understand that. If He were a prophet, He would certainly have known that Lazarus is dead; for he was dying when you went away, and he was already dead when He said the sickness is not unto death. Are you sure He said that?"

"Yes, that was what He said."

It might have been the second day after his death and He didn't come; and they watch and wait, and the third day they look for Him. "Why, it is so strange that He treats us in this way." The fourth day comes, and it is noon; yet He has not come. I can imagine that fourth day in the afternoon they receive word that Jesus is just outside the walls of Bethany with His disciples; and when He comes Martha says to Him: "If thou hadst been here, my brother had not died," and hear what gracious words fall from the lips of Jesus, "Thy brother shall live again." "Martha said unto Him, I know that He shall rise again in the resurrection, at the last day." Hear the blissful words that fall from the lips of the Son of God: "I am the resurrection and the life; he that believeth in me shall never die."

Little did Martha think that He whom she was entertaining was the Resurrection and the Life, and what a privilege it was to have such a guest! And Christ says, "Where is Mary? Go, call her." So Martha goes and calls Mary, and says, "Mary, the Master is come, and calleth for thee."

The Home in Our Hearts

Isn't there some Mary today for whom He is calling? Isn't there some unsaved Mary within these walls for whom He is calling? If there is, He wants to bind up your heart—He wants to take away your sin. And when Mary comes, she meets Him with the very same words that fell from the lips of Martha: "If thou hadst been here, my brother had not died," and Christ says, "Where have ye laid him?" And now look at Him. Those two sisters are standing near Him, and perhaps are telling Him of the last moments of Lazarus, and how their hearts had been bleeding all these four days. And when He saw them weeping, and the Jews also weeping who came with them, the heart of the Son of God was moved with compassion, and "Jesus wept." For it says, "He wept with them that wept," and the tears were streaming down His cheeks. "Then said the Jews, Behold how he loved him."

And when Jesus came to the grave He said, "Take ye away the stone." But Martha says: "He has been dead four days, and by this time it is not proper to go near him." But He commanded them to take away the stone. "Then they took away the stone from the place where the dead was laid. And Jesus lifted up his eyes, and said, Father, I thank thee that thou hast heard me. And I knew that thou hearest me always: but because of the people which stand by I said it, that they may believe that thou hast sent me." When He had thus spoken, He cried with a loud voice, "Lazarus, come forth." Someone has said, it was a good thing He called him by name, for if

He hadn't, all the dead men in that yard would have leaped up. "And he that was dead came forth, bound hand and foot with grave-clothes, and his face bound about with a napkin. Jesus saith unto them, Loose him and let him go." In the little town of Bethany now the sun is just sinking behind one of those Palestine hills; and it is now about dusk. You can see the Son of God perhaps, with Lazarus holding his arm; and they walk through the street. Ah, that was the happiest home on earth that night. I believe there was no happier home than that in Bethany that night. Isn't it the very best thing that you can do to make room for Him?

Mothers, if you will make room for Him, you will entertain the best guest, the best stranger, you ever entertained. Ah, Martha didn't know how near death was to that home when she received Christ, and, dear friends, you don't know how near death may be to you; and when death comes, what a comfort it is to have Christ to help us, to have His arms underneath us and bear us up. You need Him and had better make room for Him; and if you make room for Him here in your hearts, He will make room for you up there.

He says in that chapter which I read: "Let not your heart be troubled; ye believe in God, believe also in me. In my Father's house are many mansions; if it were not so I would have told you. I go to prepare a place for you." Instead of His disciples comforting Christ, there is Christ trying to comfort them. And now, while He is up yonder preparing a place for us, shall we not make room for Him down here? If the nations won't make room for Him; if the church won't make room for Him; if the families won't make room for Him, thanks be to God, we can make room for Him in our hearts.

We Are His Home

He says, Ye are the temples of the Holy Ghost. "Know ye not that your body is the temple of the Holy Ghost?" Will you make room for Him this afternoon? Young lady, is there room for self? Is there room for the world? Is there room for pride? Is there room for jealousy? Is there room for everyone and everything else but the Son of God? Will you turn Him away, or will you today make room for Him?

Isn't it the very best thing you can do to make room for Christ? When He made this world, He made room for us, plenty of it. He made room for Himself in our hearts, but a usurper has come. My friends, won't you let the Son of God into your hearts; and won't you let Him dwell with you?

The only room the world found for Him was just on the cross. Now, suppose He were to come here, shall He come into this hall, and shall He go through this assembly, and shall He not find room in your hearts and mine? Will your heart be full like that full inn, in Bethlehem, or will you this afternoon, just while I am speaking, say, "Lord Jesus, I make room for You in my heart"? Mother, ought not gratitude for Him who has made a place for your loved ones in heaven lead you to make room for Him? Won't you say, "Here is plenty of love; won't You come and dwell in my heart?" Just the very minute you receive Him, He will come.

Am I speaking this afternoon to some poor fallen woman? Let me say to you, He received just such, and today He will come into your heart if you will just make room for Him. How many are there in this audience today who never have thanked the Lord Jesus for the blessings He has showered upon them? And, my friends, don't let this beautiful Sabbath pass without saying, "Jesus, there shall be room in my heart for You hereafter," and then, by and by, He will receive you up yonder. If you will make room for Him here in your heart, you may be sure He will make room for you in one of His Father's mansions. Oh, this day and this hour, my friends, make room for Christ! Dear friends, don't you want Him? Today won't you make room for Him? Won't you just bow your heads, and when you pray, pray that every soul who wants Christ may come to Him?

NOTES

Joseph and Mary

Alexander Whyte (1836-1921) was known as "the last of the Puritans," and certainly his sermons were surgical as he magnified the glory of God and exposed the sinfulness of sin. He succeeded the noted Robert S. Candlish as pastor of free St. George's and reigned from that influential Edinburgh pulpit for nearly forty years. He loved to "dig again in the old wells" and share with his people truths learned from the devotional masters of the past. His evening Bible courses attracted the young people and led many into a deeper walk with God.

This sermon is taken from *Bible Characters From the Old and New Testaments*, reprinted in 1990 by Kregel Publications.

Alexander Whyte

7

JOSEPH AND MARY

SAINT MATTHEW AND Saint Luke, the first and the third
Evangelists, tell us all that we are told of Mary. They tell
us that she was the espoused wife of Joseph, a carpenter
of Nazareth, and that the Divine Call came to her after
her espousal to Joseph and before her marriage. What a
call it was, and what a prospect it opened up! No sooner
was Mary left alone of the angel than she began to realize
something of what had been appointed her, and what she
must now prepare herself to pass through. The sharp
sword that the aged Simeon afterwards spoke of with
such passion was already whetted, and was fast
approaching her devoted and exposed heart. On a thousand
sacred canvases throughout Christendom we are shown
the angel of the annunciation presenting Mary with a
branch of lily as an emblem of her beauty and as a seal of
her purity. But why has no spiritual artist stained the
whiteness of the lily with the red blood of a broken heart?
For no sooner had the transfiguring light of the angel's
presence faded from her sight than a deep and awful
darkness began to fall upon Joseph's espoused wife. Surely
if ever a suffering soul had to seek all its righteousness
and all its strength in God alone, it was the soul of the
Virgin Mary in those terrible days that followed the
annunciation. Blessed among women as all the time she
was; unblemished in soul and in body like the paschal
lamb as she was; like the paschal lamb also she was set
apart to be a divine sacrifice, and to have a sword thrust
through her heart.

Meeting Mary

Mary must have passed through many dark and
dreadful days when all she had given her to lean upon

would seem like a broken reed. "Hail, thou that art highly favored of the Lord," the angel had said to her. But all that would seem but so many mocking words to her as she saw nothing before her but an open shame, and, it might well be, an outcast's death. And, so fearfully and wonderfully are we made, and so fearful and wonderful was the way in which the Word was made flesh, that who can tell how all this may have borne on Him who was bone of her bone, and flesh of her flesh? To Him Mary was in all things a mother, as He was in all things to her a son, for hers was the face that unto Christ had most resemblance. Great is the mystery of godliness; God manifest in the flesh. A man of sorrows, and acquainted with grief. These are the beginnings of sorrows.

Joseph's Role

Joseph's part in all this is told by Saint Matthew alone. And as we read that Evangelist's particular account of that time, we see how sharp that sword which pierced Joseph's soul also. His heart was broken with this terrible trial, but there was only one course left open to him. Conclude the marriage he could not, but neither could he consent to make Mary a public example, and there was only left to him the sad step of revoking the contract and putting her away privately.

Joseph's heart must have been torn in two, for Mary had been the woman of all women to him. She had been in his eyes the lily among thorns. And now to have to treat her like a poisonous Weed—the thought of it drove him mad. Oh, why is it that whosoever comes at all near Jesus Christ has always to drink such a cup of sorrow? Truly they who are brother or sister or mother to Him must take up their cross daily. These are they who go up through great tribulation.

Mary's Journey

What a journey that must have been of Mary from Nazareth to Hebron, and occupied with what thoughts. Mary's way would lead her through Jerusalem. She may have crossed Olivet as the sun was setting. At evening she may have knelt in Gethsemane. She may have turned aside to look on the city from Calvary. What a heavy heart she must have carried through all these scenes as she went into the hill country with haste. Only two, out of God, knew the truth about Mary: an angel in heaven, and her own heart on earth. And thus it was that she fled to the mountains of Judah, hoping to find there an aged kinswoman who would receive her word and would somewhat understand her case. As she stumbled on drunk with sorrow Mary must have recalled and repeated many blessed Scriptures, well known to her indeed, but till then little understood. "Commit thy way unto the Lord; trust also in Him, and He will bring it to pass; and He shall bring forth thy righteousness as the light, and thy judgment as the noonday. Thou shalt keep them in the secret of thy presence from the pride of men; thou shalt keep them in a pavilion from the strife of tongues." Such a pavilion Mary sought and for a season found in the remote and retired household of Zacharias and Elisabeth.

Mary and Elisabeth

It is to the meeting of Mary and Elisabeth that we owe the Magnificat, the last Old Testament psalm, and the first New Testament hymn, "My soul doth magnify the Lord, and my spirit hath rejoiced in God my Savior." We cannot enter into all Mary's thoughts as she sang that spiritual song, any more than she could in her day enter into all our thoughts as we sing it. For, noble melody as her Magnificat is, it draws its deepest tones from a time that was still to come. The spirit of Christian prophecy moved her to utter it, but the noblest and fullest prophecy concerning Christ fell far short of the evangelical fulfillment.

She is a happy maiden who has a mother or a motherly friend much experienced in the ways of the human heart to whom she can tell all her anxieties; a wise, tender, much-experienced counselor, such as Naomi was to Ruth, and Elisabeth to Mary. Was the Virgin an orphan, or was Mary's mother such a woman that Mary could have opened her heart to any stranger rather than to her? Be that as it may, Mary found a true mother in Elisabeth of Hebron. Many a holy hour the two women spent together sitting under the terebinths that overhung the dumb Zacharias's secluded house. And, if at any time their faith wavered and the thing seemed impossible, was not Zacharias beside them with his sealed lips and his writing table, a living witness to the goodness and severity of God? How Mary and Elisabeth would stagger and reason and rebuke and comfort one another, now laughing like Sarah, now singing like Hannah, let loving and confiding and pious women tell.

Joseph's Discovery

Sweet as it is to linger in Hebron beside Mary and Elisabeth, our hearts are always drawn back to Joseph in his unspeakable agony. The absent are dear, just as the dead are perfect. And Mary's dear image became to Joseph dearer still when he could no longer see her face or hear her voice. Nazareth was empty to Joseph; it was worse than empty, it was a city of sepulchers in which he sought for death and could not find it. Day after day, week after week, Joseph's misery increased, and when, as his wont was, he went up to the synagogue on the Sabbath day, that only made him feel his loneliness and his misery all the more. Mary's sweet presence had often made the holy place still more holy to him, and her voice in the Psalms had been to him as when an angel sings.

On one of those Sabbaths which the exiled Virgin was spending at Hebron Joseph went up again to the sanctuary of Nazareth seeking to hide his great grief with God. And this, I feel sure, was the Scripture appointed to be read in the synagogue that day: "Ask thee a sign of the Lord thy God; ask it either in the depth, or in the height above. Therefore the Lord Himself shall give you a sign: Behold, a virgin shall conceive, and bear a son, and shall call his name Immanuel."

Joseph's heart was absolutely overwhelmed within him as he listened to that astounding Scripture. Never had ear or heart of man heard these amazing words as Joseph heard them that day. And then, when he laid himself down to sleep that night, his pillow became like a stone under his head. Not that he was cast out; but he had cast out another, and she the best of God's creatures. Ay, and she perhaps—how shall he whisper it even to himself at midnight—the virgin-mother of Immanuel! A better mother he could not have. So speaking to himself till he was terrified at his own thoughts, weary with another week's lonely labor, and aged with many weeks' agony and despair, Joseph fell asleep. Then a thing was secretly brought to him, and his ear received a little thereof. There was silence, and he heard a voice saying to him, "Joseph, thou son of David, fear not to take thee Mary thy wife, for that which is conceived in her is of the Holy Ghost." Gabriel was sent to reassure Joseph's despairing heart, to demand the consummation of the broken-off marriage, and to announce the Incarnation of the Son of God.

Did Joseph arise before daybreak and set out for Hebron to bring his outcast home? There is room to believe that he did. If he did, the two angel-chastened men must have had their own thoughts and counsels together even as the two chosen women had. And as Joseph talked with Zacharias through his writing table, he must have felt that dumbness, and even death itself, would be but a light punishment for such unbelief and such cruelty as his. But all this, and all that they had passed through since the angel came to Zacharias at the altar, only made the re-betrothal of Joseph and Mary the sweeter and the holier, with the aged priest acting more than the part of a father, and Elisabeth acting more than the part of a mother.

Mary's Gifts

For my own part, I do not know the gift or the grace or the virtue any woman ever had that I could safely deny to Mary. The divine congruity compels me to believe that all that could be received or attained or exercised by any woman would be granted beforehand, and all but without measure, to her who was so miraculously to bear, and so intimately and influentially to nurture and instruct, the Holy Child. We must give Mary her promised due. We must not allow ourselves to entertain a grudge against the mother of our Lord because some enthusiasts for her have given her more than her due. We should not fear to think too highly either of Mary's maidenly virtues, or of her motherly duties and experiences. The Holy Ghost in guiding the researches of Luke, and in superintending the composition of the Third Gospel, especially signalizes the depth and the piety and the peace of Mary's mind. At the angels' salutation she did not swoon nor cry out. She did not rush either into terror on the one hand or into transport on the other. But like the heavenly-minded maiden she was, she cast in her mind what manner of salutation this should be. And later on, when all who heard it were wondering at the testimony of the shepherds, it is instructively added that Mary kept all these things and pondered them in her heart. And yet again, when another twelve years have passed by, we find the same Evangelist still pointing out the same distinguishing feature of Mary's saintly character, "They understood not the saying which Jesus spake unto them; but His mother kept all these sayings in her heart."

Mary, Mother of All?

And, again, if we are to apply this sure principle to Mary's case, "according to your faith so be it unto you," then Mary must surely wear the crown as the mother of all them who believe on her Son. If Abraham's faith has made him the father of all them who believe, surely Mary's faith entitles her to be called their mother. If the converse of our Lord's words holds true, that no mighty work is done where there is unbelief: if we may safely reason that where there has been a mighty work done there must have been a corresponding and a cooperating faith; then I do not think we can easily overestimate the measure of Mary's faith. If this was the greatest work ever wrought by the power and the grace of Almighty God among the children of men, and if Mary's faith entered into it at all, then how great her faith must have been! Elisabeth saw with wonder and with worship how great it was. She saw the unparalleled grace that had come to Mary, and she had humility and magnanimity enough to acknowledge it.

"Blessed art thou among women: Blessed is she that believeth, for there shall be a performance of those things which were told her from the Lord." "Blessed is she that believeth," said Elisabeth, no doubt with some sad thoughts about herself and about her dumb husband sitting beside her. "Blessed is the womb that bare Thee," cried on another occasion a nameless but a true woman, as her speech bewareth her, "and Blessed be the paps that Thou hast sucked." But our Lord answered her, and said, "Yea, rather, blessed are they that hear the word of God and keep it." And again, "Whosoever shall do the will of My father in heaven, the same is My brother, and sister, and mother."

The Night of Nights

Clarence Edward Noble Macartney (1879-1957) ministered in Paterson, New Jersey, and Philadelphia, Pennsylvania, before assuming the influential pastorate of First Presbyterian Church, Pittsburgh, Pennsylvania, where he ministered for twenty-seven years. His preaching especially attracted men, not only to the Sunday services but also to his popular Tuesday noon luncheons. He was gifted in dealing with Bible biographies, and, in this respect, has well been called "the American Alexander Whyte." Much of his preaching was topical-textual, but it was always biblical, doctrinal and practical. Perhaps his most famous sermon is "Come Before Winter." The sermon I have selected is taken from *Great Nights of the Bible*, published in 1943 by Abingdon Press.

Clarence Edward Noble Macartney

8

THE NIGHT OF NIGHTS

AND THERE WERE in the same country shepherds abiding in the field, keeping watch over their flock by night (Luke 2:8).

THIS WAS THE Night of Nights! Yet that Night of Nights came down as all other nights had come down before, thousands upon thousands, ever since the first day came to a close and the first sun sank beyond the horizon, and God divided the light and the darkness, and called the light day and the darkness called he night.

The Night of Nights has come. And yet it came just as every other night before it had come. Toward the west, toward the Mediterranean Sea, the sun began to sink. Lower and lower it sank, until across the border of the western sky was one great bar of gold. Then that path of gold turned to blood red, flushing all the sky with crimson and touching earth with its fire. But in a moment the sky, so red with glory, turned to a cold ashen gray; and after that came night. To the east the mountains of Moab rise out of the shadows like colossal giants. In Bethlehem's houses mothers lay their children down to sleep. In the courtyards of the inn the camels and the cattle have lain down to rest. Here and there in some of the houses lights gleam for a moment and then go out. In the fields the sheep lie down while the shepherds sit about their fire. In the heavens above appear the same stars that had shone through all the ages, ever since God made the "stars to rule by night." Orion weaves his mystic band of Light, and the Pleiades, to the unheard music of the spheres, commence their march across the heavens.

Night had come down, just the same as night had come down in all the centuries before. Yet this is the Night of Nights! This is the night that will conquer darkness and

77

bring in the day when there shall be night no more. This is the night when they who sit in darkness shall see a great light. This is the night that shall make eternal light, for it is the night when God brought into the world Him who is the Light of the world. Yonder, in that stable of the inn, where the cattle are breathing softly in their slumber, a virgin mother has brought forth her child and laid Him in a manger. The cattle heeded it not; but over that Bethlehem manager a star will halt and angels will sing. The long journey of preparation for the redemption of the world ends on this Night of Nights. Immanuel has come!

"There were. . . . shepherds abiding in the field, keeping watch over their flock by night." The first message came to those shepherds. Not to the kings and potentates of the earth, not to the conquering soldiers, not to the rich and powerful and learned of the world, but to those shepherds as they kept watch over their flocks by night was the first Christmas sermon preached and the great tidings brought unto them that a Savior was born.

Sometimes the preacher will feel that the best he can do is to bow down in adoration before the Child, as those shepherds did, and listen to the holy song of the heavenly host, "Glory to God in the highest, and on earth peace, good will toward men!" No Christmas sermon will ever improve upon that; for in that chorus of the angels is summed up all the glory, all the beauty, and all the power of Christ and His redemption.

Poetical Luke wrote, "As the angels were gone away from them into heaven, the shepherds said one to another, Let us now go even unto Bethlehem, and see this thing which is come to pass, which the Lord hath made known unto us." Suppose we talk to ourselves with the same words and with the same music. Forget, if you can, and if you will, your sad memories, your fears, your anxieties, your distresses, your worldly thoughts and ambitions and purposes, and, as the shepherds said, "Let us now go even unto Bethlehem, and see this thing which is come to pass, which the Lord hath made known unto us."

The Prophecy and the Preparation
of the Incarnation

The great event of this Night of Nights came not without preparation, or predication and promise. In the very beginning, after the fall of man, rang out over the fallen race the first note of the Gospel, the somewhat vague and dim, yet certain, promise of a Deliverer and Savior, that the seed of the woman should bruise the head of the serpent. To Abraham the promise was given that through his descendants all nations of the earth should be blessed. Moses tells the people that a greater law-giver than he will appear in the future. Balaam, a prophet and seer outside Israel, in the rapture of his vision declares, "There shall come a Star out of Jacob, and a Scepter shall rise out of Israel." The Psalmist sings of a great King whose name shall endure forever, and who shall have the heathen for his inheritance and the uttermost parts of the earth for his possession. The prophets declare that the Desire of the Nations shall come, and that "his name shall be called Wonderful, Counselor, The mighty God, The everlasting Father, The Prince of Peace." In addition to these general promises and predications there is much that is more specific. The One who is to come will be of the tribe of Judah, of the line of David, and Bethlehem will be His birthplace. His coming will be preceded by the advent of a great prophet who shall prepare the way for Him by the preaching of repentance. Thus the Gulf Stream of Old Testament prophecy washed the shores of the remotest ages and prepared the way for the coming of the Savior.

Why did Christ not come one hundred or ten hundred years before He did, or one hundred or ten hundred years after He did? The answer is that He came in "the fullness of time," when the time was ripe, at the end of the period of preparation. "God takes a step, and the ages have elapsed."

There was a fullness of preparation among the Jewish people. In Abraham God divided the river of humanity into two streams, which flow separately until they meet again in Christ. The Jewish law proclaimed the oneness and the holiness of God. The Tabernacle and the Temple sacrifices were the shadows of the great Sacrifice of Christ upon the Cross. When the apostles went forth to preach Christ and Him crucified, wherever they went they found scattered colonies of the dispersed Jewish people, and the Jewish synagogue was the first Christian pulpit. Although Christ came to His own and His own received Him not, yet there were those who were expecting Him and waiting for Him, like the devout Simeon, who waited "for the consolation of Israel." It was not by accident, then, that on this Night of Nights the Savior was born in Bethlehem of Judea, instead of Athens or in Rome.

There was a fullness of preparation, too, in the heathen or Gentile world. The world had failed by wisdom to know God, and had confessed that failure. One of the noblest of pagan writers, Plato, said that man must take his own reason and use it as a raft on which to pass through the stormy seas, until a revelation shall come. At the time the Child was born at Bethlehem, pagan morals had sunk into a fearful climax of iniquity and shame, when men "changed the truth of God into a lie, and worshiped and served the creature more than the Creator." A dying, poisoned, hopeless world was ready for the Gospel of life and forgiveness and righteousness and hope.

The conquests of Alexander the Great had given the world an almost universal tongue, and that speech was ready for those who proclaimed and wrote the Gospel. The conquests of Rome had crushed the warring and independent nations of the world, and the Roman peace reigned when Christ was born. Otherwise, humanly speaking, Christianity would have been strangled in its cradle. But under the aegis of Roman law and government and over the splendid Roman highways the heralds of the Gospel went forth to preach Christ and Him crucified. Now had come the set time. God's hour had struck. Upon the men of that day had come the "end of the ages." Halt, Holy, Sacred Star, over Bethlehem's manger, for the long process of preparation has come to an end, and the world is ready for the angel's song!

The Manner of the Incarnation

What we have here is not the story of a God who

appeared on earth, and not the story of a man lifted up to godhead, but that God became man, that the Eternal Word became flesh and dwelt among us. This is a stupendous fact, the most overwhelming fact that can be presented to human intelligence. Even the great mind of Paul when he pondered it, exclaimed, "Great is the mystery of godliness: God was manifest in the flesh."

In the Gospels of Matthew and Luke we have the sublime story of how He came. God not only sent His only begotten Son into the world, but sent Him in a way which forever touches and thrills the heart of man. It was a way which will make all nations and all ages celebrate it to the end of time. There are, indeed, some today who claim to know better than God Himself how God ought to have come, and who say He did not come in the way the Gospels tell us He did come, conceived by the Holy Ghost and born of the Virgin Mary. The sublime narrative of the virgin birth of our Lord is a touchstone, as it were, of men's faith. The discounting or denial of the virgin birth of our Lord is inevitably linked with that indifference and coldness and dead secularism and passionless unbelief which rest as a blight upon so many of the churches and have taken the ring out of the voice of so many pulpits.

Christianity depends upon its great facts. It cannot be ethically and morally true, and at the same time historically false. In the virgin birth of our Lord we have the constituent miracle of the Christian faith. It is, indeed, a supreme and stupendous miracle, but not more so than God Himself, not more so than the soul of man, not more so than the Holy Spirit, and not more so than the Atonement of the Cross, or the Resurrection of Christ from the dead. Without this record of His birth, Christ would be the supreme enigma of the ages.

We rejoice that He came in the way that He did. All the sweet winsomeness and charm of the Christmas story gathers about His birth, the way in which He came: the Star leading on the philosophers from the East; the wonderings and musings of the guileless maid of Nazareth at what the angel had told her; the virgin mother overtaken in her great hour at Bethlehem, where there was no room for them in the inn; the manger cradle; the lowing cattle; the bowing shepherds; the echoing song of the angels. Yes, let the Star shine! Who would put it out? Let the Angel of the Lord speak to Joseph and Mary and Elisabeth and the shepherds! Who would silence his voice? Let the philosophers from the East bow down with their gifts of gold and frankincense and myrrh! Who would send them away? Let the shepherds bow at the cradle and adore! Who would stop them? Let the multitude of the heavenly host sing their holy song of good will to man and peace on earth and glory to God in the highest! Who would silence their singing?

The Purpose and the Power of the Incarnation

We are not left in doubt as to the purpose of that wonderful birth on that Night of Nights in Bethlehem's cradle. The prophets of old tell us that He will come as a Savior and to establish the Kingdom of Redemption. The Angel of the Lord said to Joseph that His name was to be Jesus, because He will save His people from their sins. The Angel of the Lord told the shepherds that unto them a Savior was born; and the song that the angels sang that night has been telling the world ever since that Christ was born that God might be glorified and that He came to bring peace to the souls of men. John said that He came to bring light and life into the world. Paul said that He came to save sinners; and Jesus Himself, the Child who was born, summed it all up by saying that He came to "seek and to save that which was lost," and that "God so loved the world, that he gave his only begotten Son, that whosoever believeth in him should not perish, but have everlasting life."

The Child who was born on this Night of Nights was born to die upon the Cross for man's salvation. Through His birth and through His death he came to seek and to save that which was lost. And through all the ages Christ has been seeking and has been finding the lost.

A light was kindled in the world that night, and ever since men who sat in darkness have seen a great light. The storms and clouds of the centuries have never been able to put it out; and still, through the dark, sad clouds of man's anarchy and sin and passion and war shines softly and beautifully, and with invincible hope, and Everlasting Light.

Christ came to bestow religious peace—peace between God and man, the peace of forgiveness—not political peace. But if all men were to receive that peace, we would have peace between the nations also. Of all the stirring, dramatic events of World War I, the one that I remember most is an event that took place on the first Christmas of the dreadful war. After months of unavailing slaughter, the colossal armies of the German Empire and France and Great Britain had fought themselves to a standstill, and now millions of their soldiers were glaring at one another out of the trenches that gashed the earth from the North Sea clear to the Alps.

In Flanders the German army lay confronting the British army. All about them the desolate, bleak country was strewn with the wreckage of the terrible struggle of these armies—blackened and ruined villages and smashed churches; jagged trunks of trees, cut down by the artillery; and everywhere a sea of yellow mud. Everywhere, too, were the dead—the dead of a month ago, the dead of a week ago, the dead of yesterday, the dead of last night. The dead were buried in the parapets of the trenches where the soldiers stood. They lay strewn in dreadful litter over No Man's Land, and clung like scarecrows to the barbed-wire defenses of both armies.

Then came Christmas Eve, the Night of Nights, the night on which our Savior was born. Standing on their platforms in the hostile trenches, the men in gray and the men in khaki watched for an attack of the enemy. But no attack came that night. At length the night passed, and the December sun rose. It was Christmas Day, the day of our Savior, the day of the Prince of Peace.

At stand-to in the morning, the British soldiers on the alert held their rifles with numb fingers and waited and watched, the frost and steam from their breath rising like a cloud on the cold winter air. Every morning they had heard a hymn of hate from the German trenches in the loud music of a burst of artillery fire. But this morning the hymn of hate did not rise. The guns back of the German trenches were silent. A great stillness came down over both lines of battle. What was to happen that Christmas morning? Suddenly the British soldiers saw three gray-clad soldiers rise out of the German trenches. This time they came without bayonets and hand grenades. Slowly, cautiously, and at first with pathetic hesitation, they approached and passed the line of their own barbed wire, and stood unprotected in No Man's Land. In a moment, before the officers realized what was happening, men by the hundreds were scrambling out of the German trenches and the British trenches, and running forward into No Man's Land.

The mud of Flanders had covered the German gray and the British khaki alike, and given to all a common uniform. The soldiers who yesterday were seeking to kill one another now put out their hands in friendly clasp and greeting, and wished one another in broken English and in broken German a Merry Christmas. Then songs were called for. The Germans responded with "Die Wacht am Rhine," and the English with "Tipperary," and the Scotch with "The Boys of Bonnie Scotland." Then the Germans began to sing, "Heilige Nacht," and "O Tannenbaum!" and the English answered with the Christmas song of England. So passed the morning and the afternoon of Christmas Day in brotherly friendship and mutual songs and the exchanging of gifts. Then the light of Christmas Day faded, and the men in gray and the men in khaki went back to their dismal trenches and took up once more the instruments of death.

Only an interlude, that was, in the chorus of war; only one incident on that far-flung battle line. But it was one of those incidents which create hope within the breast of man, which make us believe, in spite of the clouds of war and hatred that now infest our planet, that love is stronger than hate, that light is stronger than darkness, and that with the birth of Christ there came into the world a power which shall one day overcome the powers of darkness and bring in everlasting light and everlasting peace.

And, wonder of wonders, this Night of Nights was for you alone! Had you been the only one who needed a Savior, still the Night of Nights would have come. Still Christ would have been born, and still Christ would have died for you on Calvary. Will you go now with the shepherds to Bethlehem and bow before this Christ? Will you receive Him as your King and Savior? There are many who still reject Him, as they did when Christ first came. But to as many as received Him, to them gives He power to become the sons of God. Think of that! To become the sons of God! Power over sorrow, power over time, power over hate, power over temptation, power over sin, power over death!

What If Christ Had Not Come?

George W. Truett (1867-1944) pastored the First Baptist Church of Dallas, Texas, from 1897 until his death, and saw it become the largest Southern Baptist Church in the world. He was a strong man with a tender heart, and undoubtedly he was one of the greatest preachers of his time. A devoted denominational leader, he served as president of the Southern Baptist Convention and the Baptist World Alliance. This sermon is taken from *Some Vital Questions* published in 1946 by Broadman Press.

George W. Truett

9

WHAT IF CHRIST HAD NOT COME?

If I had not come . . . (John 15:22).

BEFORE COMING TO our message of the morning, I would
like to voice for you, all and each, a wish for a joyful
Christmas season. As we come again to this happy season,
may all our hearts be deeply grateful and humble, and
may we all join fervently in the prayer of Tiny Tim when
he prayed, "God bless us, everyone."

At this happy season it behooves us very wisely to
remember that the true Christmas spirit is the spirit of
unselfishness. All about us there are those whose condition
challenges our wisest and worthiest attention. There are
the needy, whichever way you turn your eyes. Who can
think of a little child being hungry and cold,
undernourished, under-privileged—or a mother in the
same plight, or any human being anywhere in like
condition—except with emotion of deepest sympathy? Then
there are the aged and the infirm, the bereaved and the
lonely. How easily can they be neglected, overlooked,
passed by! At this season there should be a summoning of
all our best thoughts to the end that all these groups
mentioned, and our fellow humanity on every side, of all
classes and conditions, may have from us the right message
in word and deed.

The apostles, when they were asked for alms, answered
by the mouth of Simon Peter: "Silver and gold have I
none; but such as I have give I thee: In the name of Jesus
of Nazareth rise up and walk." And the man rose up and
leaped for joy and went his way. That was better than to
have given him a sack filled with gold. The old proverb
from the Book of Proverbs comes to mind, namely: "A
word fitly spoken is like apples of gold in pictures of silver."
A beautiful expression, isn't it? Words are real things.

87

They can cut like a knife or they can soothe like the sweetest music. Let us through all this joyful Christmas speak the word, with our lips and with our pen, as wisely and faithfully as possible.

And now turning away from these personal expressions, let us remember that the Christmas season chronicles the chiefest event that earth has ever known, or shall ever know—the coming of the only begotten Son of God in human flesh, the God-man, to be the Savior of a sinful world.

History discloses numbers of great instances where mighty personalities came back who were supposed to have been sunk in oblivion. For example, one recalls the coming back of Napoleon. You will remember that he was banished in 1814 to Elba, and it looked like that amazingly brilliant soldier was finished. But in March 1815, barely a year later, he went back to France. He had kept close watch on events transpiring in Europe while he was away at Elba, and he knew of the unpopularity and the weakness of Louis XVIII. He was aware also of his own personal power and influence over his fellow-countrymen, so he went back to France.

The Emperor sent an army out to capture Napoleon, who alighted from his carriage and advanced toward the army without any army of his own, without even an attendant—one lone man against whom an army was sent. He went toward the army quietly, confidently; and when he was near enough, he opened his coat that the bullets of the enemy might reach his heart if they chose to fire.

Napoleon quietly said, "Frenchmen, it is your emperor." And they went wild. They kissed his hand, they fell at his feet, they picked him up and carried him on their shoulders, and they shouted until the heavens were filled with their shouts: "Vive l' empereur!" "Long live the emperor!" It was the most thrilling scene that history ever recorded of the return of one whose day-star seemed to have set.

Some years ago there was a remarkable book written by that eminent writer, William P. Stead—who late went down, you will recall, with many others, on the ill-fated *Titanic*. The book he wrote bore the title, *If Christ Should Come to Chicago*. It is a thrilling book. Imagination is set free as you read and one's deepest soul is thrilled and challenged. If Christ came to Chicago, what would He see and what would He hear and where would He go and what would He say and what would He do?

We can bring it closer and say, "If Christ came to Dallas"—today or tomorrow morning, Christmas morning—where would He go, at whose house would He stop, at whose door would He knock? Oh my soul, would He knock at my door? Would He knock at your door? Where would He go if He came to Dallas tomorrow— where would Christ go and with whom would He talk and what would He say, if He came and talked to the individual or group? If Christ came to Dallas—what a startling thought!

A more startling thought would be if Christ did not come to Dallas or to Chicago or to New York or to London, or to the Americas, or to Europe, or Asia, or Africa, or the islands of the sea—what if Christ did not come? That would be a far more startling thought! He Himself raised that question, the night before He was crucified. "If I had not come"—He used those very words. Now, let the imagination go on the wings of fancy and thought: "If Christ had not come!"

Nearly two thousand years ago He came to this world, and His spirit has made an impact deeper than that of any other personality that has ever touched this world. His spirit pervades all the realms of life. His spirit pervades literature and government and law and religion and art and music. All the spheres and realms of life have been influenced by Christ and Christianity. What if He had not come? Where would the world be, at this moment, if Christ had not come?

The World to Which He Came

Fancy the actual conditions if you will, when He came. The conditions were appalling throughout the world, nearly two thousand years ago when He came in the flesh. Three-fifths of the world was in slavery. The clanking of chains could be heard and slaves—human beings—were bought and sold as oxen, and they were beaten and bludgeoned and killed without any hesitation or compunction. There was a law among the Imperial Romans, that if a man killed an ox—just an animal—the death penalty followed for such an awful thing, but if he killed a slave, his fellow-man, it was passed by and nothing thought about it.

In ancient Greece and in Imperial Rome, slavery to an awful degree held high carnival. Masters, numbers of them, had from ten to twenty thousand human beings as their slaves. The coming of Christ sounded the death-knell of slavery, and as He and His principles are held aloft in the world, the clanking of chains of slavery will sound less and less until their echoes finally will be heard no more.

Call to mind the condition of childhood when Christ came. Often children were not welcome in the day when Jesus came. They were regarded as a burden, they were in the way in many cases. They were troublesome, they were vexing, they were unwelcome. Oh, how that is all changed! The most interesting object in the whole world is a little child. The sweetest music heard is the laughter of a little child. The most beautiful vision is the joy in the eye and on the face of a little child. Christ changed our conception of childhood when He came. He glorified the latent, measureless possibilities in a little child. Therefore, we are caring for children better all the time, with orphanages, with hospitals, with all kinds of conveniences and arrangements and improvements for their betterment.

Think of the condition of woman when Jesus came! She was a slave, she was a burden-bearer. One man would have a house full of wives, so called, and they were burden-bearers; he drove them to and fro as men drive their beasts of burden, their oxen that pulled their plows or their wagons. Christ changed all that!

I have said it again and again, and I say it again today: how any woman can keep from loving Christ, can keep from bowing before Him, from accepting Him as Lord and Master, is a mystery deeper than I can understand. The supreme champion of womanhood is Christ! There is not in the New Testament the account of one harsh word that He ever spoke to a woman. When there was dragged into His presence the poor woman who had sinned, defiled in life by her own ill-behavior, and when self-righteous men cried their bitter speech against her, Jesus wrote on the ground and then He said: "Let him that is without sin, cast the first stone." And He wrote on the ground again, and looked up and they had all gone. "Let him that is without sin, cast the first stone," but none were there to cast the stone, and gently He said to the poor woman, trembling in His presence, "Where are thine accusers? Hath no man condemned thee?" And she answered: "No man, Lord." Oh, the wonderful words of Jesus to her! "Go and sin no more." Is not that just like a divine Savior, an all-gloriously divine Savior? He has glorified womanhood, and when womanhood is lifted up, all civilization is lifted up. Marvelous transformation came to womanhood by the coming of Christ into the world.

He Changed History

But most of all, the coming of Christ Himself, this personal Christ, changed and is changing all history, even as His purposes are ripening with the rising and setting of every sun as the days come and go. Socrates, the wise man of his day, cried out in his darkness: "We look for a god, or a god-inspired man, who will teach us our duty and help us to live as we ought." The cry of men through the generations is the cry for somebody higher, better, abler than themselves.

They said to Jesus, when He came and before they understood Him, "Show us the Father and it sufficeth us." His answer was, "Have I been so long time with you, and yet hast thou not known Me, Phillip? He that hath seen Me hath seen the Father." Jesus came to reveal God. "God was in Christ reconciling the world unto himself." Jesus came that men might understand God, not as a God of cruelty, not as a God of ill, but as a God of love, of grace, of compassion, of sympathy, of every abounding interest in humanity, in all humanity. Jesus came to reveal God! "Behold, I bring you good tidings of great joy, which shall be to all people"—white and black, rich and poor, high and low, noble and ignoble, lovely and despicable, "I bring you glad tidings of great joy which shall be to all people, for unto you is born this day in the city of David, a Savior, which is Christ the Lord," said the angel. The birthday of Christ! This is the supreme event to entrance and enthrall and challenge the world forever and ever.

But look a little further. What if He had not come? If Christ had not come, where would the world be now? We would be in paganism, deep, dark, desperate paganism! The world, through all its wisdom, did not know God. Even Socrates, the wisest man of his time cried out: "We look for a god, or a god-inspired man, who will teach us our duty and help us to live like we ought to live."

If Christ had not come, we would not have the stories recorded here in this Book of His sympathy for the distressed and the distraught, and the suffering of all ages and classes and conditions of humanity. We would have no story of His pity and compassion for the leper, for the blind, for the ignorant, for the bereaved, for the brokenhearted, for the poor. God sent Christ to preach good tidings to the poor, counting that as the supreme thing. The blind receive their sight, the lepers are cleansed, the dead are raised up, and the poor have the gospel preached to them. Here is one champion for every poor man and woman in the world. He is unforgetting, unfailing, all-sufficient, and He is Christ. We would know nothing about God's care for the poor, if He had not come. We would never have heard of the story of His grace and delivering mercy in behalf of these distressed and unfortunate groups about us, if He had not come.

He Brought Us the Parables

If Christ had not come, we would not have the parables in the New Testament which so enrich and enlarge our lives. How much poorer the world would be, if we did not have that Parable of the Prodigal Son! Whose heart does not start afresh, with a sense of humility and feeling out after God, when he goes over the Parable of the Prodigal Son?

And how much poorer the world would be if we did not have the Parable of the Good Samaritan! Oh, the enlightening, the illuminating, the enlargening power of that parable! From it the question emerges, "Who is my neighbor?" Your neighbor and mine is anybody in the world who needs us. Maybe he lives close to us, maybe he lives far away, maybe he is a black man or a red man or a yellow man or a white man, of your race or another race, in sympathy with your creed, or not in sympathy with it at all. Your neighbor is anybody in the world who needs you. He may be in darkest Africa, he may be in age-old China, or in Japan, or in beaten, blungeoned India, or in America, North or South—anybody in the world who needs you is your neighbor. You cannot draw your robe around you and say, "It is nothing to me." It is something to you, and you will find it out at the judgment bar of God if not before. We are in the world, bound together in the bundle of humanity and we may not, dare not, must not, ignore the welfare of any human being in all the wide world.

We would not have all this teaching if Christ had not come. And we would not have the right estimates and appraisals of humanity if He had not come. It is easy to evaluate things as more important than human beings. It is easy to imagine that gold, stocks and bonds, houses and lands, well-filled granaries, and all such things constitute the chief values in life. Christ does not so teach. More important than all the grain that fills the granaries, and all the gold that fills the banks, more important than all this, is a human life—humble, ignorant, undeveloped though it may be, just a human life. "What shall it profit a man, if he shall gain the whole world, and lose his own soul? Or what shall a man give in exchange for his soul?" Christ, and He alone, gives us the right appraisal of humanity.

The correct test of a civilization is the kind of people that the civilization produces. What will it profit a civilization if it build towering skyscrapers and crowd its granaries with grain, and fill its banks with gold, if such civilization loses sight of the truth that yonder little child, under the wagon or shivering this morning in a cold tent, is worth more than all these material possessions that civilization can bring together? Christ gives us the right perspective, the right estimate, the right measure of a human being. Somewhere such human being is to go on, consciously and personally, forever. Wheat will not last, money will not last, houses and lands will not last. Here is a human being that is to exist forever. Christ gives us the right appraisal of humanity.

He Brought Us Atonement

If Christ had not come, we would have no adequate atonement for sin. Men were trying to fix up their own atonement, they were beating themselves, they were torturing themselves, they were offering all kinds of crude and terrible sacrifices, if haply they might ease the ache at their hearts which tormented them when there was an accusing conscience. If Christ had not come, there would have been no adequate atonement for sin.

The day that changed the world was the day of the Cross. "God forbid that I should glory, save in the cross of our Lord Jesus Christ." Jesus alone has made adequate atonement for sin; and now the person with the vilest, the lowest, the most wretched, the most terrible life in the world, can be pointed to the Cross and can be assured—if he will turn penitently to Christ who made atonement for all men, and accept Him—that person will be forgiven and will be saved. Oh, the great message in the Cross of Christ!

> In the cross of Christ I glory,
>> Towering o'er the wrecks of time.
> All the light of sacred story,
>> Gathers 'round his head, sublime.

The Cross is our hope.

If Christ had not come, we would have no door of hope beyond the grave. Men had wondered about it, speculated about it, and guessed and sighed and sobbed and gone on wondering: "Whether there be anything more, we cannot say." They said, "Whether the grave is the final chapter, we do not know." But Jesus came and comforted the brokenhearted. "Your brother shall rise again," He said to Mary and Martha. His own tears were shed with theirs out of the compassion and sympathy of His loving heart. "Thy brother shall rise again. I am the resurrection, and the life: he that believeth in me, though he were dead, yet shall he live: and whosoever liveth and believeth in me shall never die." Who can weigh the worth of these precious words from those lips divine?

The three great matters that concern mankind are life, death, eternity—and Christ alone has the only definite, clarifying, authoritative, satisfying word concerning all three. You need not be afraid of life. Trials may be in it daily for you. Do not be afraid. For He said, "I am he that liveth and was dead: and, behold, I am alive forevermore." Be not afraid of life's checkered experiences. It is given unto you, not only to believe on Christ but also to suffer for His sake. And do not be afraid of death; do not be startled nor overborne at the thought of death. The "black camel" will kneel at your gate someday and bear you away. "It is appointed unto men once to die"; do not be afraid. Only see to it that your trust is in the Christ, "who hath abolished death and brought life and immortality to light through the gospel." Cling to Him and do not be afraid of how or where you shall die; leave all that to Him, who will turn your death into a triumphant march. And do not be afraid of eternity. Christ is out there! We are going where He is. "I go to prepare a place for you. And if I go and prepare a place for you, I will come again, and receive you unto myself; that where I am, there ye may be also."

Oh, dear men and women, are you not glad that Christ came? gladder than word of man or angel could ever tell, that Christ came? Where would we be? In a pagan land. Where would you be, if Christ had not come? He is the One who gives us the right estimate of humanity, the right appraisal.

One of those poor Russian soldiers driven into battle, or a Finnish soldier fighting for his independence, or a German or an Englishman, or a Frenchman—any one of these brave men, helpless, driven by the powers superior over them, anyone is worth more than all the countries about which these men are fighting and all the assets and materials these men are grasping for. Old Dr. Knox sang the right song:

> When wilt thou save the people?
>   Oh God of mercy, when?
> Not thrones and crowns, but nations,
>   Not kings and czars but men!
> Flowers of Thy heart, Oh Lord, are they,
>   Let them not pass like weeds away;
> Their heritage is a sunless day—
>   God save the people.

And Edward Markham sang also:

> Then clear the way there, clear the way,
>   Blind kings and creeds have had their day.
> Break the dead branches from their path,
>   Our hope is in the aftermath.
> Our hope is in heroic men,
>   Christ led to build this world again—
> To this event the ages ran,
>   Make way for brotherhood, make way for man.

What is your attitude toward Christ? Oh woman, young woman, or older woman, young man or older man, happy girl or boy, how can you keep from giving your all, trustfully to Him, who alone can save? Have you done it? Will you do it now? And today, does not your heart stir with gratitude that things are as well with us as they are? That we are the recipients of such goodness and mercy? And does not every man, and woman and child in this place want to open his purse and bring a worthy offering to Christ? If He should come upon this platform now, our divine Savior, the Son of God and say: "I would be pleased if you would make a Christmas gift to Me," you would open up your purse and pour out your gifts as the Magi did of old, a gift worthy of Christ. Very well: "Inasmuch as you would do it unto Me, do it unto these!" These orphan children out at Buckner Orphans' Home, whose parents have gone on. Surely you want to make a gift to them this

Christmas time. Surely everyone would like to. Maybe you had rather write on a slip of paper that you will come in later during the week and make your gift. Let us start now, before Christmas is here and make our gift to the Buckner Orphans' Home. Let the officers come forward promptly, and take their places while the organist plays that grand old song:

> I gave my life for thee.
>> My precious blood I shed:
> That thou mightest ransomed be,
>> And quickened from the dead.
> I gave, I gave my life for Thee,
>> What has thou given for me?

Christ came in the long-ago as Savior. Christ is here now in power to save and bless and empower all who will trust Him and surrender unto Him. Christ will come again some day in person to judge the world in truth and righteousness. In this present day and hour of golden opportunity will you not take your stand with Him, wholeheartedly and without reserve? Come humbly, penitently, trustfully and He will receive you and bless you for time and eternity. Surrender to Him yourself, your heart, your all! Come now!

No Room for Christ in the Inn

Charles Haddon Spurgeon (1834-1892) is undoubtedly the most famous minister of modern times. Converted in 1850, he united with the Baptists and soon began to preach in various places. He became pastor of the Baptist church in Waterbeach in 1851, and three years later he was called to the decaying Park Street Church, London. Within a short time, the work began to prosper, a new church was built and dedicated in 1861, and Spurgeon became London's most popular preacher. In 1855, he began to publish his sermons weekly; and today they make up the fifty-seven volumes of *The Metropolitan Tabernacle Pulpit*. He founded a pastor's college and several orphanages.

This sermon is taken from *The Metropolitan Tabernacle Pulpit*, volume 8. He preached it on Sunday morning, December 21, 1862.

Charles Haddon Spurgeon

10

NO ROOM FOR CHRIST IN THE INN

And she brought forth her first-born son, and wrapped him
in swaddling clothes, and laid him in a manger; because
there was no room for them in the inn (Luke 2:7).

IT WAS NEEDFUL that it should be distinctly proven, beyond
all dispute, that our Lord sprang out of Judah. It was
necessary, also, that he should be born in Bethlehem-
Ephratah, according to the word of the Lord which he
spoke by his servant Micah. But how could a public
recognition of the lineage of an obscure carpenter and an
unknown maiden be procured? What interest could the
keepers of registers be supposed to take in two such
humble persons?

As for the second matter, Mary lived at Nazareth in
Galilee, and there seemed every probability that the birth
would take place there; indeed, the period of her delivery
was so near that, unless absolutely compelled, she would
not be likely to undertake a long and tedious journey to
the southern province of Judea. How are these two matters
to be arranged? Can one turn of the wheel effect two
purposes? It can be done! It shall be done! The official
stamp of the Roman empire shall be affixed to the pedigree
of the coming Son of David, and Bethlehem shall behold
his nativity.

A little tyrant, Herod, by some show of independent
spirit, offends the greater tyrant, Augustus. Augustus
informs him that he shall no longer treat him as a friend,
but as a vassal; and albeit Herod makes the most abject
submission, and his friends at the Roman court intercede
for him, yet Augustus, to show his displeasure, orders a
census to be taken of all the Jewish people, in readiness
for a contemplated taxation, which, however, was not
carried out till some ten years after. Even the winds and
waves are not more fickle than a tyrant's will; but the

Ruler of tempests knows how to rule the perverse spirits of princes.

The Lord our God has a bit for the wildest war horse, and a hook for the most terrible leviathan. Autocratical Caesars are but puppets moved with invisible strings, mere drudges to the King of kings. Augustus must be made offended with Herod; he is constrained to tax the people; it is imperative that a census be taken; nay, it is of necessity that inconvenient, harsh, and tyrannical regulations should be published, and every person must repair to the town to which he was reputed to belong; thus, Mary is brought to Bethlehem, Jesus Christ is born as appointed, and, moreover, he is recognized officially as being descended from David by the fact that his mother came to Bethlehem as being of that lineage, remained there, and returned to Galilee without having her claims questioned, although the jealousy of all the women of the clan would have been aroused had an intruder ventured to claim a place among the few females to whom the birth of Messiah was now by express prophecies confined. Remark here the wisdom of a God of providence, and believe that all things are ordered well.

When all persons of the house of David were thus driven to Bethlehem, the scanty accommodation of the little town would soon be exhausted. Doubtless friends entertained their friends till their houses were all full, but Joseph had no such willing kinsmen in the town. There was the caravansary, which was provided in every village, where free accommodation was given to travelers; this, too, was full, for coming from a distance, and compelled to travel slowly, the humble couple had arrived late in the day. The rooms within the great brick square were already occupied with families; there remained no better lodging, even for a woman in travail, than one of the meaner spaces appropriated to beasts of burden. The stall of the ass was the only place where the child could be born. By hanging a curtain at its front, and perhaps tethering the animal on the outer side to block the passage, the needed seclusion could be obtained, and here, in the stable, was the King of Glory born, and in the manger was he laid.

My business this morning is to lead your meditations to the stable at Bethlehem, that you may see this great sight—the Savior in the manger, and think over the reason for this lowly couch—"because there was no room for them in the inn."

I. I shall commence by remarking that

There Were Other Reasons Why Christ Should Be Laid in the Manger.

1. I think it was intended thus *to show forth his humiliation*. He came, according to prophecy, to be "despised and rejected of men, a man of sorrows and acquainted with grief"; he was to be "without form or comeliness," "a root out of a dry ground." Would it have been fitting that the man who was to die naked on the cross should be robed in purple at his birth? Would it not have been inappropriate that the Redeemer who was to be buried in a borrowed tomb should be born anywhere but in the humblest shed, and housed anywhere but in the most ignoble manner? The manger and the cross standing at the two extremities of the Savior's earthly life seem most fit and congruous the one to the other. He is to wear through life a peasant's garb; he is to associate with fishermen; the lowly are to be his disciples; the cold mountains are often to be his only bed; he is to say, "Foxes have holes, and the birds of the air have nests, but the Son of Man hath not where to lay his head"; nothing, therefore, could be more fitting than that in his season of humiliation, when he laid aside all his glory, and took upon himself the form of a servant, and condescended even to the meanest estate, he should be laid in a manger.

2. By being in a manger *he was declared to be the king of the poor*. They, doubtless, were at once able to recognize his relationship to them from the position in which they found him. I believe it excited feelings of the tenderest brotherly kindness in the minds of the shepherds, when the angel said—"This shall be a sign unto you; you shall find the child wrapped in swaddling-clothes and lying in a manger." In the eyes of the poor, imperial robes excite no affection, but a man in their own garb attracts their

confidence. With what pertinacity will working-men cleave to a leader of their own order, believing in him because he knows their toils, sympathizes in their sorrows, and feels an interest in all their concerns. Great commanders have readily won the hearts of their soldiers by sharing their hardships and roughing it as if they belonged to the ranks. The King of Men who was born in Bethlehem, was not exempted in his infancy from the common calamities of the poor, nay, his lot was even worse than theirs. I think I hear the shepherds comment on the manger-birth, "Ah!" said one to his fellow, "then he will not be like Herod the tyrant; he will remember the manger and feel for the poor; poor helpless infant, I feel a love for him even now, what miserable accommodation this cold world yields its Savior; it is not a Caesar that is born today; he will never trample down our fields with his armies, or slaughter our flocks for his courtiers, he will be the poor man's friend, the people's monarch; according to the words of our shepherd-king, he shall judge the poor of the people; he shall save the children of the needy."

Surely the shepherds, and such as they—the poor of the earth, perceived at once that here was the plebeian king; noble in descent, but still as the Lord hath called him, "one chosen out of the people." Great Prince of Peace! the manger was thy royal cradle! Therein wast thou presented to all nations as Prince of our race, before whose presence there is neither barbarian, Scythian, bond nor free; but thou art Lord of all. Kings, your gold and silver would have been lavished on him if ye had known the Lord of Glory, but inasmuch as ye knew him not he was declared with demonstration to be a leader and witness to the people. The things which are not, under him shall bring to nought the things that are, and the things that are despised which God hath chosen, shall under his leadership break in pieces the might, and pride, and majesty of human grandeur.

3. Further, in thus being laid in a manger, he did, as it were, *give an invitation to the most humble to come to him.* We might tremble to approach a throne, but we cannot fear to approach a manger. Had we seen the Master

at first riding in state through the streets of Jerusalem with garments laid in the way, and the palm-branches strewed, and the people crying, "Hosanna!" we might have thought, though even the thought would have been wrong, that he was not approachable. Even there, riding upon a colt the foal of an ass, he was so meek and lowly, that the young children clustered about him with their boyish "Hosanna!"

Never could there be a being more approachable than Christ. No rough guards pushed poor petitioners away; no array of officious friends were allowed to keep off the importunate widow of the man who clamored that his son might be made whole; the hem of his garment was always trailing where sick folk could reach it, and he himself had a hand always ready to touch the disease, an ear to catch the faintest accents of misery, a soul going forth everywhere in rays of mercy, even as the light of the sun streams on every side beyond that orb itself. By being laid in a manger he proved himself a priest taken from among men, one who has suffered like his brethren, and therefore can be touched with a feeling of our infirmities. Of him it was said, "He doth eat and drink with publicans and sinners"; "this man receiveth sinners and eateth with them." Even as an infant, by being laid in a manger, he was set forth as the sinner's friend. Come to him, ye that are weary and heavy-laden! Come to him, ye that are broken in spirit, ye who are bowed down in soul! Come to him, ye that despise yourselves and are despised of others! Come to him, publican and harlot! Come to him, thief and drunkard! In the manger there he lies, unguarded from your touch and unshielded from your gaze. Bow the knee, and kiss the Son of God; accept him as your Savior, for he puts himself into that manger that you may approach him. The throne of Solomon might awe you, but the manger of the Son of David must invite you.

4. Methinks there was yet another mystery. You remember, brethren, that this place was *free to all*; it was an inn, and please to remember the inn in this case was not like our hotels, where accommodation and provision must be paid for. In the early and simple ages of the

world every man considered it an honor to entertain a stranger; afterwards, as traveling became more common, many desired to shift the honor and pleasure upon their neighbors; wherefore should they engross all the dignity of hospitality? Further on still, some one person was appointed in each town and village, and was expected to entertain strangers in the name of the rest; but, as the ages grew less simple, and the pristine glow of brotherly love cooled down, the only provision made as the erection of a huge square block, arranged, in rooms for the travelers, and with lower stages for the beasts, and here, with a certain provision of water and in some cases chopped straw for the cattle, the traveler must make himself as comfortable as he could. He had not to purchase admittance to the caravansary, for it was free to all, and the stable especially so. Now, beloved, our Lord Jesus Christ was born in the stable of the inn to show how free he is to all comers. The Gospel is preached to every creature and shuts out none. We may say of the invitations of Holy Scripture,

> "None are excluded hence but those
>   Who do themselves exclude;
> Welcome the learned and polite,
>   The ignorant and rude.
>
> Though Jesus' grace can save the prince,
>   The poor may take their share;
> No mortal has a just pretense
>   To perish in despair."

Class exclusions are unknown here, and the prerogatives of caste are not acknowledged. No forms of etiquette are required in entering a stable; it cannot be an offense to enter the stable of a public caravansary. So, if you desire to come to Christ you may come to him just as you are; you may come *now*. Whosoever among you hath the desire in his heart to trust Christ is free to do it. Jesus is free to you; he will receive you; he will welcome you with gladness, and to show this, I think, the young child was cradled in a manger.

We know that sinners often imagine that they are shut out. Oftentimes the convicted conscience will write bitter things against itself and deny its part and lot in mercy's stores. Brother, if *God* has not shut you out, do not shut yourself out. Until you can find it written in the Book that you may not trust Christ; till you can quote a positive passage in which it is written that he is not able to save you, I pray you take that other word wherein it is written— "He is able to save unto the uttermost them that come unto God by him." Venture on that promise: come to Christ in the strength and faith of it, and you shall find him free to all comers.

5. We have not yet exhausted the reasons why the Son of Man was laid in a manger. It was at the manger that *the beasts were fed*; and does the Savior lie where weary beasts receive their provender, and shall there not be a mystery here? Alas, there are some men who have become so brutal through sin, so utterly depraved by their lusts, that to their own consciences every thing manlike has departed, but even to such the remedies of Jesus, the Great Physician, will apply. We are constantly reading in our papers of men who are called incorrigible, and it is fashionable just now to demand ferociously, that these men should be treated with unmingled severity.

Some few years ago all the world went mad with a spurious humanity, crying out that gentleness would reform the brutal thief whom harsh punishments would harden hopelessly; now the current has turned, and everybody is demanding the abandonment of the present system. I am no advocate for treating criminals daintily; let their sin bring them a fair share of smart; but if by any means they can be reformed, pray let the means be tried. The day will come when the paroxysm of this garroting fever is over, we shall blush to think that we are frightened by silly fears into a dangerous interference with a great and good work which hitherto has been successfully carried on. It is a fact that under the present system, which (abating some faults that it may be well to cure) is an admirable one, crime is growing less frequent, and the class of gross offenders has been materially lessened. Whereas in 1844, 18,490 convicts were transported, in 1860 the corresponding number was 11,533, and that notwithstanding the increase of the population. The ticket-of-leave system, when the public would employ the convicts and so give them a chance of gaining a new character, worked so well that little more than one percent in a year were re-convicted, and even now only five percent per annum are found returning to crime and to prison. Well, now, if the five percent receive no good, or even become worse, ought we not to consider the other ninety-five, and pause awhile before we give loose to our vengeance and exchange a Christian system of hopeful mercy for the old barbarous rule of unmitigated severity?

Beware, fellow-citizens, beware of restoring the old idea that men can sin beyond hope of reformation, or you will generate criminals worse than those which now trouble us. The laws of Draco must ever be failures, but fear not for the ultimate triumph of plans which a Christian spirit has suggested. I have wandered from the subject—I thought I might save some from the crime of opposing true philanthropy on account of a sudden panic; but I will return at once to the manger and the babe. I believe our Lord was laid in the manger where the beasts were fed, to show *that even beast-like men may come to him and live.* No creature can be so degraded that Christ cannot lift it up. Fall it may, and seem to fall most certainly to hell, but the long and strong arm of Christ can reach it even in its most desperate degradation; he can bring it up from apparently hopeless ruin. If there be one who has strolled in here this morning whom society abhors, and abhors himself, my Master in the stable with the beasts presents himself as able to save the vilest of the vile, and to accept the worst of the worst even now. Believe on him and he will make you a new creature.

6. But as Christ was laid where beasts were fed, you will please to recollect that after he was gone *beasts fed there again.* It was only his presence which could glorify the manger, and here we learn that if Christ were taken away *the world would go back to its former heathen darkness.* Civilization itself would die out, at least that

part of it which really civilizes man, if the religion of Jesus could be extinguished. If Christ were taken away from the human heart, the most holy would become debased again, and those who claim kinship with angels would soon prove that they have relationship to devils. The manger, I say, would be a manger for beasts still, if the Lord of Glory were withdrawn, and we should go back to our sins and our lusts if Christ should once take away his grace and leave us to ourselves. For these reasons which I have mentioned, methinks, Christ was laid in a manger.

II. But still the text says that he was laid in a manger because there was no room for him in the inn, and this leads us to the second remark, that

There Were Other Places Besides the Inn Which Had No Room for Christ.

The palaces of emperors and the halls of kings afforded the royal stranger no refuge? Alas! my brethren, seldom is there room for Christ in palaces! How could the kings of earth receive the Lord? He is the Prince of Peace, and they delight in war! He breaks their bows and cuts their spears in sunder; he burns their war-chariots in the fire. How could kings accept the humble Savior? They love grandeur and pomp, and he is all simplicity and meekness. He is a carpenter's son, and the fisherman's companion. How can princes find room for the new-born monarch? Why he teaches us to do to others as we would that they should do to us, and this is a thing which kings would find very hard to reconcile with the knavish tricks of politics and the grasping designs of ambition.

O great ones of the earth, I am but little astonished that amid your glories, and pleasure, and wars, and councils, you forget the Anointed, and cast out the Lord of All. There is no room for Christ with the kings. Look throughout the kingdoms of the earth now, and with here and there an exception it is still true—"The kings of the earth stand up, and the rulers take counsel together, against the Lord and against his Anointed." In heaven we shall see here and there a monarch; but ah! how few;

indeed a child might write them. "Not many great men after the flesh, not many mighty are chosen." State-chambers, cabinets, throne-rooms, and royal palaces, are about as little frequented by Christ as the jungles and swamps of India by the cautious traveler. He frequents cottages far more often than regal residences, for there is no room for Jesus Christ in regal halls.

"When the Eternal bows the skies
    To visit earthly things,
With scorn divine he turns his eyes
    From towers of haughty kings.
He bids his awful chariot roll
    Far downward from the skies,
To visit every humble soul
    With pleasure in his eyes."

But there were *senators, there were forums of political discussion, there were the places where the representatives of the people make the laws*, was there no room for Christ there? Alas! my brethren, none, and to this day there is very little room for Christ in parliaments. How seldom is religion recognized by politicians! Of course a State-religion, if it will consent to be a poor, tame, powerless thing, a lion with its teeth all drawn, its mane all shaven off, and its claws all trimmed—yes, that may be recognized; but the true Christ and they that follow him and dare to obey his laws in an evil generation, what room is there for such? Christ and his gospel—oh! this is sectarianism, and is scarcely worthy of the notice of contempt. Who pleads for Jesus in the senate? Is not his religion, under the name of sectarianism, the great terror of all parties? Who quotes his golden rule as a direction for prime ministers, or preaches Christ-like forgiveness as a rule for national policy? One or two will give him a good word, but if it be put to the vote whether the Lord Jesus should be obeyed or not, it will be many a day before the *ayes* have it. Parties, policies, place-hunters, and pleasure-seekers exclude the Representative of Heaven from a place among representatives of Earth.

Might there not be found some room for Christ *in what*

is called good society? Were there not in Bethlehem some people who were very respectable, who kept themselves aloof from the common multitude; persons of reputation and standing—could not they find room for Christ? Ah! dear friends, it is too much the case that there is no room for him in what is called good society. There is room for all silly little forms by which men choose to trammel themselves; room for the vain niceties of etiquette; room for frivolous conversation; room for the adoration of the body; there is room for the setting up of this and that as the idol of the hour, but there is to little room for Christ, and it is far from fashionable to follow the Lord fully. The advent of Christ would be the last thing which society would desire; the very mention of his name by the lips of love would cause a strange sensation. Should you begin to talk about the things of Christ in many a circle, you would be tabooed at once. "I will never ask that man to my house again," so-and-so would say—"if he must bring his religion with him." Folly and finery, rank and honor, jewels and glitter, frivolity and fashion, all report that there is no room for Jesus in their abodes.

But is there not room for him *on the exchange*? Cannot he be taken to the marts of commerce? Here are the shop-keepers of a shop-keeping nation—there is not room for Christ here? Ah! dear friends, how little of the spirit, and life, and doctrine of Christ can be found here! The trader finds it inconvenient to be too scrupulous; the merchant often discovers that if he is to make a fortune he must break his conscience. How many there are—well, I will not say they tell lies directly, but still, still, still—I had better say it plainly—they do lie indirectly with a vengeance. What sharp practice some indulge in! What puffery and falsehood! What cunning and sleight of hand! What woes would my Master pronounce on some of you if he looked into your shop-windows, or stood behind your counters. Bankruptcies, swindlings, frauds are so abundant that in hosts of cases there is no room for Jesus in the mart or the shop.

Then there are *the schools of the philosophers*, surely they will entertain him. The wise men will find in him incarnate wisdom; he, who as a youth is to become the teacher of doctors, who will sit down and ask them questions and receive their answers, surely he will find room at once among the Grecian sages, and men of sense and wit will honor him. "Room for him, Socrates and Plato! Stoics and Epicurians give ye way; and you, ye teachers of Israel, vacate your seats; if there is no room for this child without your going, go; we must have him in the schools of philosophy if we put you all forth." No, dear friends, but it is not so; there is very little room for Christ in colleges and universities, very little room for him in the seats of learning.

How often learning helps men to raise objections to Christ! Too often learning is the forge where the nails are made for Christ's crucifixion; too often human wit has become the artificer who has pointed the spear and made the shaft with which his heart should be pierced. We must say it, that philosophy, falsely so called, (for true philosophy, if it were handled aright, must ever be Christ's friend) philosophy, falsely so called, has done mischief to Christ, but seldom has it served his cause. A few with splendid talents, a few of the erudite and profound have bowed like children at the feet of the Babe of Bethlehem, and have been honored in bowing there, but too many, conscious of their knowledge, stiff and stern in their conceit of wisdom, have said, "Who is Christ, that we should acknowledge him?" They found no room for him in the schools.

But there was surely one place where he could go—it was *the Sanhedrim*, where the elders sit. Or could he not be housed in the priestly chamber where the priests assemble with the Levites? Was there not room for him in the temple or the synagogue? No, he found no shelter there; it was there, his whole life long, that he found his most ferocious enemies. Not the common multitude, but the priests were the instigators of his death; the priests moved the people to say, "Not this man, but Barabbas." The priests paid out their shekels to bribe the popular voice, and then Christ was hounded to his death. Surely there ought to have been room for him in the Church of his own people; but there was not.

Too often in the priestly church, when once it becomes recognized and mounts to dignity, there is no room for Christ. I allude not now to any one denomination, but take the whole sweep of Christendom, and it is strange that when the Lord comes to his own his own receives him not. The most accursed enemies of true religion have been the men who pretended to be its advocates. It is little marvel when bishops undermine the popular faith in revelation; this is neither their first nor last offense. Who burned the martyrs, and made Smithfield a field of blood, a burning fiery furnace, a great altar for the Most High God? Why, those who professed to be anointed of the Lord, whose shaven crowns had received episcopal benediction. Who put John Bunyan in prison? Who harried the Covenanters upon the mountains? Who, Sirs, but the professed messengers of heaven and priests of God? Who have hunted the baptized saints in every land, and hunt them still in many a Continental state? The priests ever; the priests ever; there is no room for Christ with the prophets of Baal, the servants of Babylon. The false hirelings that are not Christ's shepherds, and love not his sheep, have ever been the most ferocious enemies of our God and of his Christ. There is no room for him where his name is chanted in solemn hymns and his image lifted up amid smoke of incense. Go where ye will, and there is no space for the Prince of Peace but with the humble and contrite spirits which by grace he prepares to yield him shelter.

III. But now for our third remark,

The Inn Itself Had No Room for Him;

and this was the main reason why he must be laid in a manger.

What can we find in modern times which stands in the place of the inn? Well, there is *public sentiment free to all.* In this free land, men speak of what they like, and there is a public opinion upon every subject; and you know there is free toleration in this country to everything— permit me to say, toleration to everything but Christ. You will discover that the persecuting-spirit is now as much abroad as ever. There are still men at whom it is most fashionable to sneer. We never scoff at Christians now-a-days; we do not sneer at that respectable title, lest we should lose our own honor; we do not now-a-days talk against the followers of Jesus under that name. No; but we have found out a way of doing it more safely.

I would give not a farthing for your religion, nay, not even the turn of a rusty nail, unless you will sometimes be persecuted and misunderstood. If God's Word be true, every atom of it, then we should act upon it; and whatsoever the Lord commands, we should diligently keep and obey, remembering that our Master tells us if we break one of the least of his commandments, and teach men so, we shall be least in his kingdom. We ought to be very jealous, very precise, very anxious, that even in the minutiae of our Savior's laws, we may obey, having our eyes up to him as the eyes of a servants are to their mistresses. But if you do this, you will find you are not tolerated, and you will get the cold shoulder in society.

A zealous Christian will find as truly a cross to carry now-a-days, as in the days of Simon the Cyrenian. If you will hold your tongue, if you will leave sinners to perish, if you will never endeavor to propagate your faith, if you will silence all witnessing for truth, if, in fact, you will renounce all the attributes of a Christian, if you will cease to be what a Christian must be, then the world will say, "Ah! that is right; this is the religion we like." But if you will believe, believe firmly, and if you let your belief actuate your life, and if your belief is so precious that you feel compelled to spread it, then at once you will find that there is no room for Christ even in the inn of public sentiment, where everything else is received. Be an infidel, and none will therefore treat you contemptuously; but be a Christian, and many will despise you. "There is no room for him in the inn."

How little room is there for Christ, too, *in general conversation*, which is also like an inn. We talk about many things; a man may now-a-days talk of any subject he pleases, no one can stop him and say, "There is a spy catching your words; he will report you to some central authority." Speech is very free in this land; but ah! how little room is there for Christ in general talk! Even on Sunday afternoon how little room there is for Christ in some professed Christian's houses. They will talk about ministers, tell queer anecdotes about them—perhaps invent a few, or, at least, garnish the old ones, and add to them, and make them a little more brilliant; they will talk about the Sunday school, or the various agencies in connection with the Church, but how little they say about Christ! And if someone should in conversation make this remark, "Could we not speak upon the Godhead and manhood, the finished work and righteousness, the ascension, or the second advent or our Lord Jesus Christ," why we should see many, who even profess to be followers of Christ, who would hold up their heads and say, "Why, dear, that man is quite a fanatic, or else he would not think of introducing such a subject as that into general conversation." No, there is no room for him in the inn; to this day he can find but little access there.

I address many who are working-men. You are employed among a great many artisans day after day; do you not find, brethren—I know you do—that there is very little room for Christ *in the workshop*? There is room there for everything else; there is room for swearing; there is room for drunkenness; there is room for lewd conversation; there is room for politics, slanders, or infidelities; but there is no room for Christ. Too many of our working men think religion would be an encumbrance, a chain, a miserable prison to them. They can frequent the theater, or listen in a lecture-hall, but the house of God is too dreary for them. I wish I were not compelled to say so, but truly in our factories, workshops, and foundries, there is no room for Christ. The world is elbowing and pushing for more room, till there is scarce a corner left where the Babe of Bethlehem can be laid.

As for the inns of modern times—who would think of finding Christ there? Putting out of our catalogue those hotels and roadside houses which are needed for the accommodation of travelers, what greater curse have we than our taverns and saloons? What wider gates of hell?

Who would ever resort to such places as we have at the corners of all our streets to find Christ there? As well might we expect to find him in the bottomless pit! We should be just as likely to look for angels in hell, as to look for Christ in a gin palace! He who is separate from sinners, finds no fit society in the reeking temple of Bacchus. There is no room for Jesus in the inn. I think I would rather rot or feed the crows, than earn my daily bread by the pence of fools, the hard-earnings of the poor man, stolen from his ragged children, and his emaciated wife. What do many publicans fatten upon but the flesh, and bones, and blood, and souls of men? He who grows rich on the fruits of vice is a beast preparing for the slaughter. Truly, there is no room for Christ among the drunkards of Ephraim. They who have anything to do with Christ should hear him say—"Come ye out from among them, and be ye separate; touch not the unclean thing and I will receive you, and be a father unto you, and ye shall be my sons and daughters." There is no room for Christ now-a-days even in the places of public resort.

IV. This brings me to my fourth head, which is the most pertinent, and the most necessary to dwell upon for a moment:

Have You Room for Christ?

As the palace, and the forum, and the inn, have no room for Christ, and as the places of public resort have none, have *you* room for Christ? "Well," says one, "I have room for him, but I am not worthy that he should come to me." Ah! I did not ask about worthiness; have you room for him? "Oh," says one, "I have an empty void the world can never fill!" Ah! I see you have room for him. "Oh! but the room I have in my heart is so base!" So was the manger. "But it is so despicable!" So was the manger a thing to be despised. "Ah! but my heart is so foul!" So, perhaps, the manger may have been. "Oh! but I feel it is a place not at all fit for Christ!" Nor was the manger a place fit for him, and yet there was he laid. "Oh! but I have been such a sinner; I feel as if my heart had been a den of beasts and devils!" Well, the manger had been a place where beasts had fed.

Have you room for him? Never mind what the past has been; he can forget and forgive. It matters not what even the present state may be if you mourn it. If you have but room for Christ, he will come and be your guest. Do not say, I pray you, "I hope *I shall have* room for him"; the time is come that he shall be born; Mary cannot wait months and years. Oh! sinner, if you have room for him let him be born in your heart today.

"Today if ye will hear his voice harden not your hearts as in the provocation." "Today is the accepted time; today is the day of salvation." Room for Jesus! Room for Jesus now! "Oh!" says one, "I have room for him, but will he come?" Will he come indeed! Do you but set the door of your heart open, do but say, "Jesus, Master, all unworthy and unclean I look to you; come, lodge within my heart," and he will come to you, and he will cleanse the manger of your heart, nay, will transform it into a golden throne, and there he will sit and reign forever and forever.

Oh! I have such a free Christ to preach this morning! I would I could preach him better. I have such a precious loving Jesus to preach, he is willing to find a home in humble hearts. What! are there no hearts here this morning that will take him in? Must my eye glance round these galleries and look at many of you who are still without him, and are there none who will say, "Come in, come in"? Oh! it shall be a happy day for you if you shall be enabled to take him in your arms and receive him as the consolation of Israel! You may then look forward even to death with joy, and say with Simeon—"Lord, now lettest thou thy servant depart in peace, according to thy word, for mine eyes have seen thy salvation."

My Master wants room! Room for him! Room for him! I, his herald, cry aloud, Room for the Savior! Room! Here is my royal Master—have you room for him? Here is the Son of God made flesh—have you room for him? Here is he who can forgive all sin—have you room for him? Here is he who can take you up out of the horrible pit and out of the miry clay—have you room for him? Here is he who when he comes in will never go out again, but abide with you forever to make your heart a heaven of joy and bliss for you—have you room for him? 'Tis all I ask. Your emptiness, your nothingness, your want of feeling, your want of goodness, your want of grace—all these will be but room for him. Have you room for him? Oh! Spirit of God, lead many to say, "Yes, my heart is ready." Ah! then he will come and dwell with you.

> "Joy to the world the Savior comes,
> The Savior promised long;
> Let every heart prepare a throne
> And every voice a song."

V. I conclude with the remark, that if you have room for Christ, then from this day forth remember

The World Has No Room for You;

for the text says not only that there was no room for him, but look—"There was no room *for them*"—no room for Joseph, nor for Mary, any more than for the babe. Who are his father, and mother, and sister, and brother, but those who receive his word and keep it? So, as there was no room for the blessed Virgin, nor for the reputed father, remember henceforth there is no room in this world for any true follower of Christ. There is no room for you to take your *ease*. No, you are to be a soldier of the cross, and you will find no ease in all your life-warfare. There is no room for you to sit down *contented with your own attainments*, for you are a traveler, and you are to forget the things that are behind, and press forward to that which is before; no room for you *to hide your treasure* in, for here the moth and rust doth corrupt; no room for you *to put your confidence*, for "Cursed is he that trusteth in man, and maketh flesh his arm." From this day there will be no room for you in *the world's good opinion*—they will count you to be an offscouring; no room for you in the world's *polite society*—you must go without the camp, bearing his reproach. From this time forth, I say, if you have room for Christ, the world will hardly find room of *sufferance* for you; you must expect now to be laughed at; now you must wear the fool's cap in men's esteem; and your song must be at the very beginning of your pilgrimage.

"Jesus, I thy cross have taken,
All to leave and follow thee;
Naked, poor, despised, forsaken,
Thou from hence my all shall be."

There is no room for you in the worldling's love. If you expect that everybody will praise you, and that your good actions will all be applauded, you will be quite mistaken. The world, I say, has no room for the man who has room for Christ. If any man love the world, the love of the Father is not in him. "Woe unto you when all men speak well of you." "Ye are not of the world, even as Christ is not of the world." Thank God, you need not ask the world's hospitality. If it will give you but a stage for action, and lend you for an hour a grave to sleep in, 'tis all you need; you will require no permanent dwelling-place here, since you seek a city that is to come, which has foundations; whose builder and maker is God. You are hurrying through this world as a stranger through a foreign land, and you rejoice to know that though you are an alien and a foreigner here, yet you are a fellow citizen with the saints, and of the household of God.

What say you, young soldier, will you enlist on such terms as these? Will you give room for Christ when there is to be henceforth no room for you—when you are to be separated forever, cut off from among the world's kith and kin mayhap—cut off from carnal confidence forever? Are you willing, notwithstanding all this, to receive the traveler in? The Lord help you to do so, and to him shall be glory forever and ever. Amen.

The Mystery of Godliness

Arthur Tappan Pierson (1837-1911) served
Presbyterian churches in New York, Michigan, Indiana
and Pennsylvania, and had a worldwide ministry
promoting missions and evangelism. He helped to organize
the Student Volunteer Movement, served as a consulting
editor for the *Scofield Bible*, and authored many books on
Bible study, missions and the victorious Christian life.
When Charles Spurgeon became ill in 1891, Pierson filled
the pulpit for a year and again in 1893, after Spurgeon
died and before the church called Thomas Spurgeon from
New Zealand. This sermon was preached at the
Metropolitan Tabernacle in the autumn of 1891. It is taken
from Pierson's book *The Gospel: Its Heart, Heights and
Hope*, reprinted in 1978 by Baker Book House, Grand
Rapids, Michigan.

Arthur Tappan Pierson

11

THE MYSTERY OF GODLINESS

> But if I tarry long, that thou mayest know how thou oughtest to behave thyself in the house of God, which is the church of the living God, the pillar and ground of the truth. And without controversy great is the mystery of godliness: God was manifest in the flesh, justified in the Spirit, seen of angels, preached unto the Gentiles, believed on in the world, received up into glory (1 Timothy 3:15,16).

THE PUNCTUATION OF our English Bible is not assured by divine inspiration, inasmuch as there are no punctuation points, properly so called, in the original Scriptures. The punctuation is the device of the translators in hope to make plainer to the ordinary reader what is the meaning. These two verses present us an example of disputed punctuation. Bengel, the author of the Gnomon of the New Testament, remarks that not until the sixteenth century were the words, "pillar and ground of the truth," ever referred to the church of God, but always to the doctrine which follows; and it seems that the better punctuation of these two verses concludes the fifteenth verse with the words, "living God." "These things I write unto thee, hoping to come unto thee shortly, but if I tarry long, that thou mayest know how thou oughtest to behave thyself in the house of God, which is the church of the living God." And then a new sentence should begin: "The pillar and ground of the truth, and, without controversy, great, is the mystery of godliness." This would refer the words "pillar and ground of the truth" to the great doctrine which follows, which embraces the whole system of "piety" or gospel truth which centers in the incarnation of our blessed Lord Jesus Christ.

There is much reason to believe, likewise, that this is a portion of an original apostles' creed, older by far than the oldest confession of faith known to the church of Christ.

In those early days of the apostolic church, when they had, as yet, no written Scriptures of the New Testament, and no formula or confessions of faith, it was very desirable, if not necessary, that there should be brief expressions of great Christian doctrines, or fact, which could be so arranged as to be readily committed to memory, and which were doubtless recited either as hymns or as confessions among early disciples. There are seven cases in the New Testament in which these fragments of some original confession seem to be found, as "this is a faithful saying"; that is, "This is a saying which is full of the faith, or expresses the faith." And if you will examine into those seven cases, you will find, in every instance, some great, some central truth of redemption, set before us. For example, in the ninth verse of the fourth chapter, we have one of these faithful sayings which the apostle declares to be "worthy of all acceptation," namely, that "godliness is profitable unto all things, having promise of the life that now is, and of the life that is to come. For therefore we both labor and suffer reproach, because we trust in the living God, who is the Savior of all men, specially of those that believe."

Its Form

The conviction that this text is a fragment of some original confession of faith, is confirmed by the poetic form in which it appears. The ancient Hebrews used very largely what we call parallelism, a rhythm and a rhyme of thought rather than a rhythm and a rhyme of words; as, for instance, in the Book of the Proverbs: "A wise son maketh a glad father, but a foolish son is the heaviness of his mother," where it is the sentiment in the two clauses that corresponds, rather than mere rhyme or rhythm or meter; and so here you have this same poetic construction. And you will observe that there are three couplets here, each consisting, of course, of two members—

"God was made manifest in the flesh:
Justified in the Spirit."
"Seen of angels:

Preached among the nations."
"Believed on in the world:
Received up into glory."

There is a concession of the fact that this is a mystery,
without controversy great. We may as well concede the
mystery where even the Holy Ghost does not dispute it. It
is said, sometimes, that the Bible is full of mysteries, and
men make it an excuse for not receiving the truths of the
Word of God because they are mysterious; but one of the
marks that the Bible is the Word of God is found in the
presence of these same mysteries. "What man knoweth
the things of man save the spirit of man which is in him?
Even so the things of God knoweth no man but the Spirit
of God," says Paul, in the second chapter of First
Corinthians. And what is the idea? The ability perfectly
to understand the work or workmanship of any man
implies in me or in you an equality with that man.

Here is a watch, a very dainty and delicate and intricate
machine or piece of mechanism. Now, if you can
understand every part of that watch, why every jewel is
in its place, why certain materials are used in it, and why
everything is in the form and in the place which it
occupies—if every detail of the construction of that watch
is understood by you, then, if you had the time, and the
implements, and the materials, you could make another
watch like unto it. The ability absolutely to understand
God, implies an equality with God. Because he is as far
above us as the heaven is higher than the earth, therefore
are his thoughts far beyond the reach of our thoughts,
and we can no more take God into our comprehension,
than the very smallest flower-cup, that a drop of dew fills,
could take in the vastness of the ocean.

One of the seals of God upon his word is inscrutable
mystery. It is true that the mystery never concerns
questions of duty, but always concerns questions of a
speculative rather than a practical character. There are
secret things that belong unto the Lord our God, but all
the things of his law belong to the revealed things that
are for the practical guidance of ourselves and our children.
And because there never was another being, and never

will be another being, like the God-Man, who was not simply God in man, or man in God, but a unique person, the God-Man, two natures in one person—because we have never had before, and shall never have again, another being like him, and so cannot become familiar with, and by familiar contact accustomed to, the fact of such a person—he must always remain an inscrutable mystery. Let us concede it, and confess it, and abandon all idea that we shall, by our philosophy, ever fathom the depth of it.

Then, again, besides the obvious mystery of the incarnation, it is here declared to be the pillar and prop of the truth. The first word indicates that it is *central*, and the other word indicates that it is *vital*. If you took away the pillars of this house, these galleries would fall immediately upon the floor below. When Samson put his arms about the pillars of Dagon's temple, and withdrew them from their standing-place, the whole building came down upon the heads of the worshipers. This great doctrine embodied in this confession is both central in the system of doctrine, and vital to the doctrine itself. Just as soon as a man begins to doubt that Jesus Christ was God manifest in the flesh, look out for his creed. His whole system of theology is doomed to tumble down and bury him beneath its ruins. He begins by this departure from the truth, but all other departures from truth will logically follow; for if you take away the central and vital pillar and prop of the whole redemptive scheme, you have no longer the doctrine that is according to godliness.

A Comprehensive Doctrine

This, which is thus a mysterious doctrine and a central doctrine, is also a very comprehensive doctrine. Suppose that we examine these three couplets:

"God was made manifest in the flesh:
Justified in the Spirit.
Seen of angels:
Preached among the Gentiles.
Believed on in the world:
Received up into glory."

This statement of this great doctrine covers everything from Christ's birth in the inn, at Bethlehem, to his ascension and assumption of the throne of the universe at the right hand of the Father. There is nothing that concerns his career, from the manger to the throne, from birth to resurrection and ascension—glory, that is not involved in this brief confession of faith.

This somewhat lengthy introduction is needful to clear the way for the application of this theme. And to make it so simple and easy of apprehension, that even a child may be able to get at the vital truth of it, allow me to say that these three couplets may serve to answer three practical questions: First, *who was he?* second, *why was he?* and third, *where is he?*

I. First, Who was he? It is declared, in the first of these couplets, that he was—

> "God manifest in the flesh,
> Justified in the Spirit."

Here our attention is called to the fact that he was man on the one side, and God on the other—God in man, and man in God, the God-Man.

His humanity was the more manifest thing, though "God was manifest in the flesh." We use the word "manifest" oftentimes of that which is very clear, very obvious, and very unmistakable; but not in that sense are we to understand the word "manifest" in this text. The fact is that Jesus Christ was *veiled* in the flesh rather than revealed in the flesh. The flesh was the form which God took for manifestation; but the flesh actually became an obscuring medium. It was his humanity that impressed men, and not his divinity. Even his disciples who walked with him closely for three years, seem to have had doubts of his divinity to the very last, because that which impressed them most, and which was most apparent, was his humanity, and not the divine nature that dwelt in him. As Van Oosterzee finely says, Jesus Christ came in the garments of our humanity, and it was only now and then, when this robe of his humanity was swept aside, as the mantle of some general-in-chief is sometimes swept aside when he is reviewing the troops of a great army, that you might at times discover the imperial star of universal royalty shining and glittering upon his breast. Jesus Christ lived among men as a man. He seemed to be a man, though the greatest and grandest of men; and, because his humanity was manifest rather than his divinity, it became necessary that he should be justified in the Spirit; that is to say, that by the Holy Ghost dwelling within him and working through him, it should be manifest that he was more than man—that he was God.

How was he justified in the Spirit?

In the first place, long before he came on earth, the Spirit justified him in advance as the Son of God and the Messiah of men, by the wonderful utterances of prophecy. Three hundred and thirty-three distinct predictions about our Lord and Savior are found between Genesis and Malachi, entering into the minutest details of prediction, telling when he should be born, and where he should be born, and under what circumstances, and outlining all the great facts of his life, death, resurrection and ascension. And the whole canon of the Old Testament Scriptures closed four hundred years before Christ appeared on the earth, and the collected body of Old Testament Scriptures was in the hands of the Jews at least two hundred years before Christ was born.

A Prophetic Picture

This prophetic argument is a mighty argument, both for the divinity of Christ and for the inspiration of the Word of God. We may compare the Holy Ghost and prophets of old to a body of artists completing a picture. At first, in the third chapter of Genesis, is a simple outline, on a broad scale, without coloring, of him who, as the seed of the woman, was to bruise the serpent's head. Then came the fuller prophecies of the period of Moses and the period of David, and the period of the prophets, the earlier and the later; and each prophet, as he comes to the great canvas on which the Holy Ghost had outlined the person and work of Jesus Christ, adds a new feature—here and there a touch of drawing, or a touch of color, until, when

Malachi lays down his pen, there stands a complete and majestic portrait of the coming Messiah, like the perfect picture of some great hero of the future. And then, when the evangelists take up their pens to write the simple story of Christ's life and death and resurrection and ascension, you find that the picture from the evangelists exactly corresponds to the picture from the prophets.

The portrait of the future Messiah, made by the prophets under the guidance of the Holy Spirit, is the picture of the Messiah who has already come, as furnished by the evangelists in the New Testament. Nay, you may take the prophetic portrait, and put it over the portrait by the evangelists, and find that the lines of the features exactly correspond throughout. That is the way that in advance the Spirit justified the coming Messiah as one that was to be the Son of God, the mighty worker, the everlasting Lord.

Then, when Christ came, the Spirit justified him by works such as man never wrought, and words such as man never spoke. A great deal has been said in these days about the miracles of Jesus Christ. Often we forget that these were not simply miracles of wisdom, or miracles of power; but they were, above all, miracles of love, miracles of benevolence, unselfish ministry to the wants of men; and how blind, therefore, and how hard, must have been the whole nature of those who said, "He worketh miracles and casteth out devils through Beelzebub, the prince of the devils." Even though Satan might have had the mightiest power among men, can you imagine him using that power in works of mercy and love, and healing and recovery? There were never such words of wisdom as Jesus spoke; and there were never such works of mercy and love, as well as power and wisdom, as he wrought. And so the Holy Ghost testified to him during his life.

Resurrection Power

And then came the greatest of all the Spirit's testimonies; for Paul says, in the fourth verse of the first chapter of the Epistle to the Romans, that He was "declared to be the Son of God with power"—that is with especial power—"by the resurrection from the dead." Where all men cease to exercise activity and influence, there the ministry of Jesus Christ practically began the period of its greatest power. Men go into the grave, and we put up by their sepulchers in our cemeteries the broken pillar, the quenched fire, and the plucked flower, as the symbols to express the idea that life has been broken off, and light has been put out, and hope has been blasted. But when you come to the sepulcher of Jesus Christ, there the pillar receives its crown and its capital: there the fire just begins to burn in its celestial glory: there the flower bursts into the fullness of its bloom.

The Holy Ghost declared the Son of God to be the Son of God, with power, when he raised him from the dead, so that he broke the bonds of death, and burst the bars of the tomb, and when, on the third day, he came forth in open triumph over death and "him that hath the power of death, that is the devil."

And we must make more of the resurrection of Jesus Christ. Paul says, in the fifteenth chapter of 1 Corinthians, "If Christ be not risen, your faith is vain and our preaching vain, and ye are yet in your sins." We sometimes say that Jesus Christ, by his death, delivers us from the wrath to come. I am not sure that that is an exact and full statement. We are told in the Epistle to the Romans that he was delivered over for our offenses, but raised again for our justification. If he had not been raised, the penalty of death would still have been upon him as upon a transgressor of the law. There would have been no sign that his mediation for man was accepted by the Father; but when he rose from the dead, and came forth from his prison in the grave, as man's substitute accepted by God and walking in the universe like a free man, it was evident that God had accepted his sacrifice and his substitution, and that man in him was delivered from his offenses.

II. Now, let us examine the second of these couplets: "Seen of angels"—or messengers, which the word means— "preached among the nations." This answers the question, "Why was Jesus Christ?" Why was all this manifestation of God in the flesh and justification of the Godhead in him by the Spirit? This couplet answers. Inasmuch as Christ's death for our sins, and resurrection for our justification, were necessary to the salvation of mankind, it was necessary also that he should be preached among the Gentiles as the world's Savior. I think that the first part of this second couplet includes, in the word "messengers," not only angels, but men. His resurrection must be made an established fact beyond any reasonable doubt; and so Paul, in the fifteenth chapter of 1 Corinthians, gives us an account of the various appearances of Christ after he was risen from the dead, enumerating them in order, and closing with the appearance to himself, to whom Christ appeared as to one born out of due time; and he tells us that He was seen by about five hundred brethren at once, of whom the greater part remained at the time that he was writing, though some had fallen asleep.

You perceive with what infinite pains God made clear the fact that Jesus Christ had risen from the dead, so that there is no fact of all history that is more abundantly affirmed and confirmed by many and various witnesses than the fact of Christ's resurrection. For forty days he continued with the disciples, eating and drinking with them after he was risen from the dead, and instructing them in the matters pertaining to his kingdom. The theory that Christ simply appeared to the disciples like a phantom, or a ghost, or an illusion, will not hold for a moment; for ghosts and phantoms do not discourse about spiritual mysteries, and do not eat and drink and continue to accompany people intelligently in converse with them for forty days. I say again, there is no event of all history more abundantly established by many infallible proofs than the resurrection of Jesus Christ from the dead.

And so he was preached among the Gentiles, or nations, as the world's Savior. We take up the witness of these great facts from those who, before us, have taken the testimony of those that preceded them; and so there is an apostolic succession, of the truest and grandest sort, that reaches back, through generations of believers, and ages of church history, to the time when the disciples, who themselves met Christ repeatedly after his resurrection, gave their witness to this great fact.

III. Now, we come to the third couplet. Where is he?

"Believed on in the world:
Received up into glory."

I want this to be the climax of this text and of this discourse; and may God help me, first of all, to speak in his name, and then help you to hear and heed this testimony of the precious Word of God.

"Believed on in the world:
Received up into glory,"

or "caught up into glory." Christ is here and he is also there. He is here, because he is in every believer's heart; he is there, because he is exalted at the right hand of God to be a Prince and a Savior. And let us not fail to notice that Jesus Christ is not only in the whole body of believers, but he is in every believing soul. We sometimes lose sight of what may be called the individuality of redemption, by referring all the wonderful things said about Jesus, and his indwelling by the Spirit, to the collective body of the disciples.

He is not only in the great body of believers—the church—but he is in the body of everyone who believes. Paul and Peter say not only that we are stones in a temple and are built up into one spiritual house, but Paul asks, "Know ye not that your body is the temple of the Holy Ghost?"—not the Body of Christ, not the whole body of believers, but "*your body* is the temple of the Holy Ghost, and the Spirit dwelleth in you." And what does Jesus Christ say in that magnificent promise in the twenty-third verse of the fourteenth of John? "If any man love me he will keep my words, and my Father will love him, and we will come *unto him* and *make our abode with him*." "With *him*"; that is to say, with every individual believer.

If you love and obey Christ, if your heart goes out to him in holy reverence and supreme obedience, if you open all the avenues of your nature to the entering in of the Son of God by his Word and by his Spirit, he and the Father, as well as the Holy Ghost—the triune God—come down from the high and holy place which they inhabit, and in your humble and contrite heart make their personal dwelling. There is not a man, a woman, a child, who believes in Jesus Christ, who is not a temple of the Holy Ghost. And, as God looks down upon such believers he values you more, individually, as his temple than the most magnificent cathedral ever erected. St. Paul's and Westminster Abbey, and the cathedrals of Cologne and Strasburg, Florence and Milan, and St. Peter's at Rome— all these costly and sumptuous buildings are as nothing to him, who more prizes a humble, contrite, believing soul as his abode than the stateliest of all temples erected from the foundation of the world. And he would have you to appreciate this fact, and with deep thanksgiving to recognize it; that, if you in your heart worship and obey your Master and Lord, he is in your heart as an indwelling power and presence.

Each of you can, therefore, test this gospel for yourself. You need not be at the mercy of other people and their testimony. Go into your secret place, commune with your Father who is in heaven, through Jesus Christ your Lord, and, by the power of the Holy Ghost, let God unfold to you his presence and his power within you. That is the standing miracle of the ages. That is the personal and perpetual testimony unto God. That is the great apologetic of Christianity. That is the whole system of "evidences" concentrated in a believing soul—the portable evidence of Christianity.

I have but one more of these phrases to consider, and that lifts us to the highest heaven of praise and glory and adoring worship. "Caught up into glory." What does that mean? Let us not refer this to Christ's resurrection. It refers to a grander event—the event of his ascension! We make far too little of this glorious fact—our Lord's ascension. His incarnation was wonderful; his temptation in the desert was wonderful; his passion in Gethsemane was wonderful; his death on the cross was wonderful; his resurrection from the grave was stupendous; but his ascension overtops them all in majesty, divinity, power, and glory. And, because the ascension of our Lord is so little thought of, even by ministers of Christ and believing disciples, I pray God that I may speak as becomes this august theme in these closing words.

Now, what is it that constitutes the ascension of Christ—his rapture into the glory—as, thus far, the consummation of all the wonders of redemption?

Let me say very briefly that, ever since Jesus Christ came into this world, there has been a deadly conflict going on between the prince of this world and the Prince of the Kingdom of God. We cannot stop now to trace the successive stages of this conflict. Every time that the devil met Jesus Christ in deadly encounter it was more desperate and more daring on his part, and his defeat more terrible and overwhelming; for Jesus Christ not only overcame him in every instance, but with more and more overwhelming victory.

When Christ ascended up on high, if there ever was an occasion when Satan would have desired to prevent such a consummation, it was then; for remember that, when Jesus Christ came down in the incarnation, he brought God down to man; but when he ascended, he bore man up to God. If Satan would fain have prevented God coming down to man, how much more would he have prevented man ascending to God! Remember, he tempted Adam in the garden, and the slime of the serpent has been over all human powers and pleasures ever since. The fairest flowers of Eden may remain among us, but they are wilted and withered. The paths of paradise may be dimly seen, but they are covered with the tracks of the serpent. But, mark the stupendous mystery—the very humanity that in the first Adam had fallen was, in the ascension, mounting to the throne of glory! The very humanity that Satan had trod down in the dust of wreck and ruin in Eden, was, in the second Adam, mounting above all principalities and powers and dominions and every name that is named, and ascending the steps of the throne of the universe to sit down with God in the equality of his imperial reign. And, when that cloud hid from the disciples' eyes the ascending Savior, who can tell what conflict between the prince of the power of the air and the ascending Christ, that cloud may also have hidden from mortal eye?

I think I see in the Word of God some indications of this conflict, not only in the passage already quoted, but in that found in the fourth chapter of the Epistle to the Ephesians: "When he ascended up on high he led captivity captive and gave gifts unto men." It needs but the smallest acquaintance with ancient history to understand this language. It is drawn from the customs of great generals, when they had accomplished a wonderful victory; they entered the city of Rome, in triumphal procession, with captives behind them laden with golden chains; and it sometimes occurred that the very generals that had defeated the Roman army, were themselves in turn defeated, and brought in chains to Rome to be sacrificed.

Now, Jesus Christ at the grave had been triumphed over, for a time, by the power of Satan, the great destroyer; and then, when he broke the bands of death asunder, and triumphed over Satan, he in turn trod him down in awful defeat; and now the very Satan that had triumphed over Christ at the grave, and made him his captive for a time, he was leading, as in chains, up into the very presence of the august God. The ascension was Christ's triumphal procession, when a multitude of captives, the devil at the head, and all the demons that were associated with him in his work of darkness, were in chains, brought low, and the great General-in-Chief, the imperial Captain of our salvation, with his white plume waving, mounted to the throne of God, holding all these fallen angels captive in his train. Then, like an ancient general in his triumphal procession, he distributed his largess of gifts to men; and, as he led Satan and his bands captive, he flung down from the portals of heaven the golden coin of the kingdom, in the gift of the Holy Ghost. And so you and I are enriched today by this celestial currency, because the largess of his ascension triumph has been rained down upon us.

I think I begin to understand something of what the twenty-second, twenty-third and twenty-fourth Psalms mean. The twenty-second Psalm is the psalm of his death. The twenty-third Psalm is the psalm of his burial. The twenty-fourth Psalm is the psalm of his ascension, and it closes with this magnificent challenge: "Lift up your heads,

O ye gates; and be ye lift up, ye everlasting doors; and the King of glory shall come in. Who is this King of glory? The Lord strong and mighty, the Lord mighty in battle. Lift up your heads, O ye gates; even lift them up, ye everlasting doors; and the King of glory shall come in. Who is this king of glory? The Lord of hosts, he is the King of glory." It is the appeal to the heavenly gates to unfold on their golden hinges, and let the King of glory, mighty over all foes, enter and take final possession of his throne.

There may be some, even in this audience of believers, who have never admitted the King of glory into the innermost recesses of the heart, and I entreat you in the name of our ascended and glorified Savior, to speak to your own hearts this day, and say, Lift up your heads, O gates of my soul; even be lifted up, ye doors of my heart; and let the King of glory come in. Who is the King of glory? The Lord strong and mighty to overcome the power of your sin, as he has overcome already its penalty, and then to banish the presence of sin by-and-by. Lift up your heads, O ye gates of my soul, and be ye lift up, ye doors of my heart. Let the King of glory come in. Who is this King of glory? The Lord of hosts, he is the King of glory!

NOTES

The Guidance of the Star

Henry Parry Liddon (1829-1890) belonged to the High
Church school of the Anglican Church. Ordained in 1853,
he served in two brief pastorates and as vice-principal of
a school. He moved to Oxford and there preached to large
crowds at St. Mary's and Christ Church. He is perhaps
best known for his Bampton Lectures, *The Divinity of Our
Lord and Savior Jesus Christ*. From 1870 to his death, he
was canon of St. Paul's Cathedral, London, which he sought
to make into an Anglican preaching center to rival Charles
Spurgeon's Metropolitan Tabernacle. This sermon, slightly
abridged, comes from *Christmastide in St. Paul's*,
published in 1891 by Longmans, Green & Co., London.

Henry Parry Liddon

12

THE GUIDANCE OF THE STAR

> Now when Jesus was born in Bethlehem of Judea in the days of Herod the king, behold, there came wise men from the East to Jerusalem, saying, Where is He that is born King of the Jews? for we have seen His star in the East, and are come to worship Him (Matthew 2:1,2).

THE FESTIVAL OF the Epiphany must be deemed of very high importance by a believing and thoughtful Christian. It does not merely commemorate one of the most beautiful incidents of our Lord's Infant Life. It asserts one of the most fundamental and vital features of Christianity; the great distinction, in fact, between Christianity and Judaism. The Jewish religion was the religion of a race. If a man was born of the seed of Abraham and was circumcised on the eighth day, he was in covenant with God. If the blood that flowed in his veins was Greek or Roman, he was a stranger to the covenant of promise; he could at best, in some favorable circumstances, attain an outward connection with the religious system of Judaism, as did a proselyte of the gate. It was the consideration of this which led St. Paul to ask whether God was the God of the Jews only; whether he was not God of the Gentiles also. Was a merely national religion like this a full unveiling of the Mind of the common Father of the human family? Was His Eye ever to rest in love and favor only on the hills and valleys of Palestine? Was there to be no place in His Heart for those races who lay east and west and north and south of the favored region? Or was the God of Israel, like the patron-deities of the heathen world, the God of Israel in such sense that Israel could lastingly monopolize His interest, His protection, His love; that heathendom, lying in darkness and in the shadow of death, would live on in it forever, without a hope of being really lightened by His Countenance, or being admitted to share His embrace?

135

It could not be. The Jewish revelation of God contained within itself the secret and the reason of its vanishing by absorption into the brighter light which should succeed it. Just as the Apostle points out, when writing to the Hebrews, that the Jewish ritual, when closely scrutinized, was seen to be pregnant with the sentence of its own abolition since it foreshadowed that perfect work of the One Atoning Victim, which it could not itself achieve; so much more did that glorious and blessed revelation of God's Being and character, which the Law and the Prophets taught so fully and so variously to the chosen people, make it impossible that God should not manifest Himself to others. How would His mercies have been over all His works; how would it have been true that He was Lord of all, if all, save one favored race, were to be forever outside His kingdom of righteousness? No; Judaism, as a religious system, read the sentence of its coming disappearance in the handwriting of its greatest seers and rulers. "All nations whom Thou hast made shall come and worship Thee, O Lord, and shall glorify Thy Name." "All the ends of the world shall remember themselves and be turned unto the Lord; and all the kingdoms of the nations shall worship before Him: for the kingdom is the Lord's." "It is a light thing," so runs the prophetic message to Messiah, "that Thou shouldest be My Servant to raise up the tribes of Jacob, and to restore the preserved of Israel: I will also give Thee for a Light unto the Gentiles, that Thou mayest be My Salvation unto the ends of the earth." Or—to omit much else to the same effect—"There shall be a Root of Jesse, and He that shall rise to reign over the Gentiles; in Him shall the Gentiles trust."

These anticipations were not really realized when, during the two or three centuries before our Lord, educated pagans at Alexandria and elsewhere began to take a deeper interest in the Jewish religion, and to detect in it a higher truth than they had known before. The first step to the fulfillment of the predictions of David and of Isaiah was made when the Wise Men crossed the desert on their visit to the Cradle at Bethlehem. That visit opens a new era in the religious history of the world. We Gentiles of today, who have gathered here to worship our Divine Redeemer, owe all that we hope from Him in time and in eternity, to that grace which led those Gentiles of old to come to Christ's light, those "kings to the brightness of His rising." Let us, then, inquire more particularly what lessons this remarkable event has to teach us.

How God Speaks to Us

This visit of the Wise Men shows us, first of all, how variously God speaks to us; how many are the voices whereby He calls us, if we will, out of darkness, whether of the mind or of the heart, into His marvelous light. He uses a language to each which each can understand. It may be childish, even unintelligible, in the ears of other men; but it has a substantive value for us, if we will only hear it.

The home of the Wise Men was probably in Persia. They belonged to the order or caste of Magi, who for many centuries represented the current wisdom of the East. They were looking out for some Deliverer from evils of which they felt the pressure, without being able to define and describe them. The historians Tacitus and Suetonius tell us that a rumor was current throughout the East which pointed to Judea as the birthplace of men who would rule the world; and this rumor would have gathered strength from the vague longings for a Savior which were widely felt by heathens as well as by Jews. As St. Paul says that the Jewish Law, like the heathen slave whose duty it was to lead his master's sons to school, led Israel to Jesus Christ, the true Teacher of humanity; so the natural law, written in the hearts of the heathen, did a kindred work. It made the heathen conscious of that moral evil from which they could not free themselves; it made them long for deliverance. Thus many minds throughout heathendom were looking out for tokens of a heavenly Visitant, and their inquiries took the direction which their education and habits of thought suggested. Men who in the West would have inquired of oracles, tried when in the East to read the language of the stars. The opinion that Balaam's prophecy of the Star of Jacob was still a sufficiently powerful tradition to shape the yearnings of these sages, is somewhat precarious; they simply tried to find in the heavens an answer to the profound moral yearnings within themselves.

We know that astrology is a false science. It is impossible to connect the movements and appearances of the heavenly bodies with the affairs of men in such a degree and manner as astrologers have supposed. There are moral as well as other reasons for this conviction; but astrology, being, as it is, false, would not have largely swayed the lives of men unless it had been based upon a truth. This truth is, that the material universe is the servant of the moral, that is to say, of man. The stars are the work of the Perfect Moral Being; and His Nature is the measure of the relative worth and of the several purposes of the creatures to which He has given existence.

This truth is stated in the first chapter of Genesis, in which other creatures are represented as existing, not simply in obedience to some law of production, but for the sake of man. Joshua fell back upon this truth when the lengthened day enabled him to complete his victory of Beth-horon. Deborah recognized this truth when she sang how the stars in their courses had fought against Sisera. And it was this truth which ennobled the speculations of the Eastern sages. While in the East they saw the star of the King of the Jews.

They saw, probably, at first, one of the fixed stars, to which they were led, in the course of their inquiry, to attach this specific value; and as it shone out on them night by night over their western horizon, they determined to walk in the direction from which it shone, or, as we should say, to follow it. They followed it, accordingly, day by day; night by night they gazed wistfully at it, and then rose to follow it again; they gazed and followed, and so they crossed the desert and reached the city to which even the heathen East had learned to ascribe an exceptional sanctity. And as their coming became known at gatherings of the priesthood, and in the palace of the king, they learned how an ancient prophecy had ruled that He Whom they sought would be born in Bethlehem.

And now the Divine guidance took another and a miraculous form. Between their Eastern home and Jerusalem, it was probably a fixed star to which they were led to attach a special meaning; but between Jerusalem and Bethlehem, St. Matthew's language is too explicit not to oblige us to suppose that they were guided, not by their own impressions, but by an object moving independently of themselves; probably by a meteor which appeared to them to be identical with the star they had before observed, and which, from the nature of its movement, must have been preternatural. "When they had heard the king, they departed; and, lo, the star, which they saw in the East, went before them, till it came and stood over where the young Child was. And when they saw the star, they rejoiced with exceeding great joy."

It has been said, by way of objection to St. Matthew's history, that God would not thus have appeared to sanction a false science by leading souls through its supposed guidance to a knowledge of His Blessed Son. But, apart from what has been said as to the truth which underlies astrology, this criticism proceeds upon a mistaken estimate of the nature of human events. In human events the good and the evil, the true and the false, are so closely linked, that the latter often serve for the point of transition to the former. God does not break this chain of events when He would act upon mankind; and thus we behold speculative error working itself out into the light of truth, and superstition paving the way for faith. Constantly has this been witnessed in the history of conversions to Christianity, whether of individuals or of nations; here a false philosophy, as in St. Augustine's case, there a stupid superstition, sometimes by contrast, sometimes by sympathy, becomes all unconsciously to itself, and even against its natural drift and purpose, a preparation for the Gospel.

Truly it has been said that man can more easily understand the Magnificence of God than the depths of His Condescension. If God had been all that His critics would have made Him, He would have been too careful of His dignity to help us out of our errors or our sins. We, in our shortsightedness, constantly prescribe conditions to Him under which alone, as we think, souls can be brought to know and to love Him. One man cannot believe that any can be brought to God unless the reasoning powers have been cultivated up to a particular point. Another insists upon the supreme importance of warm feelings; another cannot understand a love of God which is dissociated from the sense of beauty and cares nought for art. Thus we men speak, each looking at the heavens, as our petty individual horizons bound them. But He, the Universal Father, Whose mighty Heart is open to all of us, Who knows each one of us as being what each really is, Who distinguishes with unerring accuracy that which matters little to our endless peace from that which matters much—He sooner or later has a word for all of us. The star which one man sees and follows is to another like any other star in the heavens. The influence of a friend, some public occurrence, a sentence of Holy Scripture, a family trouble, the arguments of a book, suddenly arrest attention. The soul reads a meaning where it saw none before. Are we to find fault with God for dealing with us as we are? Is He wrong, then, for taking this man's reason captive, and saying little to his affections; or for winning that man's heart, and leaving his imagination uninterested; or for stimulating the imagination of a third to apprehend His glory with vivid energy, while the faculty which understands the worth of an argument is dormant or almost unfelt?

Hush! Let us trust Him to do right in this matter. It is well that, as individuals, we are as little capable of controlling the flow and impulse of His grace as of regulating the rain and the sunshine. He may seem to violate our narrow rules; but He has a larger Heart than these rules allow for, and the day will come when we shall understand Him.

Truth Must Be Sought for

This history teaches us also that truth, if it is to be grasped in its fullness, must be *sought* for, and that earnestly. The Wise Men had a little stock of truth to start with; a shadowy tradition, a vague presentiment. This was their excellence and their safety: they made the most of what had been given them. Like the faithful servant in the parable, their pound gained ten pounds. They did not put away from them what they knew or felt, as if it were only a scruple or a superstition, and not worth considering. They applied themselves first to the studies from which, as they believed, they could obtain an answer, and next to carrying into practice, by a serious and painful effort, the further duties which the answer imposed on them.

They studied till they found the star; they left the homes, in which they were surrounded by wealth and consideration, to journey into a distant land; they reached its capital, and having ascertained that the object of their search was to be found beyond, they set out again. They might too easily have given up inquiry when it became evident that to complete it would be costly and fatiguing; they might have persuaded themselves that if Jerusalem did not reward their efforts it was folly to travel on to a provincial town, and that they had better return. They succeeded because they did not yield to these temptations. They persevered until they had found.

This is a consideration which needs to be insisted on. To neglect it is to run the risk of religious presumption on the one hand, or of religious despair on the other.

It has been said that "English people often appear to take it for granted that religious knowledge comes, whether by accident or as a matter of course, to every one who takes any interest in religion." Yet no man of prudence, who has not given much time to reading law, would feel that he could express an opinion on a difficult legal question; he would expose himself by doing so to ridicule, if to nothing worse. No sensible man, who had not studied human frame, and the laws which act upon it, would commit himself, offhand, to an opinion upon the nature of an alarming disease, or upon the true methods of treating it; he would fear to endanger a human life by his ignorant presumption. But too often, in religious matters, we have no doubt about our perfect capacity for deciding, without any hesitation, any question that may come before us, although we have never given it serious attention, and really resemble a blind man discussing art in a picture-gallery, or, rather, a child playing marbles on the edge of a precipice. We assume that, somehow, we can form opinions, and act on them, and persuade others to act on them, without absurdity or danger.

"Yes," you reply, "but does not God send His Holy Spirit to teach those that ask Him?" Doubtless He does. But He does not so bestow that precious Gift as to make it needless for us to exert ourselves, or to use the other aids which He has given us. The star, with its high significance, was a gift of God. But the Wise Men did not think that the sight of the star rendered any further effort unnecessary, or that they would do some dishonor to the Heavenly Giver if they followed the path along which He seemed to lead. There is no spirituality in religious torpor. It is an Apostle who cries, "If we live in the Spirit, let us also walk in the Spirit."

Still less can the light of natural conscience be pleaded as a reason for making no effort to know and serve its author. Most true it is that God does give to every man, at the outset of life, a certain elementary knowledge of Himself. The star which might lead to the cradle of the Divine Infant shines at some time into every human conscience. God endows us all, without exception, with the sense and perception of a distinction and a law; the distinction between right and wrong, whatever right and wrong may be; and the law of obedience to right, when once it is discovered. And if a man makes the most of this endowment, instead of shunning or scorning or doing it violence; if he allows himself to reflect that such inward legislation implies a Lawgiver, and to search for other traces of His Presence and action; then, assuredly, is he on the way to learn more.

Men often ask why when St. Paul preached at Athens or Corinth nearly two thousand years ago, or when a missionary preaches today in India or Africa, one person listens with thankful interest, while another turns away in anger or disgust. And the answer may be, that the one has made the most of the gift of natural light within him, while the other has not. The one has dwelt on the faint glimmer of truth, rejoicing in it, longing that it might become brighter, wondering whence it came, and what can be known of its Author; and therefore, when a messenger from the Author, who can show trustworthy credentials, comes to tell him more, he listens and believes. The other has felt haunted and disquieted by the inward light; he has wished it extinguished. And who does not know that such wishes will in the end prevail?

God leaves those who will away with Him to the darkness which they prefer. And therefore, when Christ's Apostle speaks to such an one, he speaks a language which the soul has no ears to hear. Micah's prophecy of the coming glories of Bethlehem would have seemed to the Wise Men the wildest nonsense, had they not seen and followed the star in the East. Our knowledge of high truth depends on our fidelity to lower truths; on our making the most of whatever we may know at starting, and making good each step in our advance.

This is the law of God's kingdom to the end of time. "Whosoever hath, to him shall be given; and whosoever hath not, from him shall be taken, even that which he seemeth to have." And to "have" is to make the most of that which God gives; to possess with conscious joy at the possession; to seek that which lies beyond whatever we already possess. "If thou criest after knowledge," says the Wise Man, "and liftest up thy voice for understanding; if thou seekest for her as silver, and searchest for her as for hid treasures; then shalt thou understand the fear of the Lord, and find the knowledge of God."

Here also is a safeguard, not only against presumption, but against despair. God gives some light at some time to all; and if we follow it, it will lead us on. Here is a man who has been thrown early in life into a society where every objection that can be urged against Revelation has been continually repeated. He has fairly lost his way. It seems to him, for the moment, that if you are honest and educated, and if you are not a clergyman and so committed to a religious view of things, you must admit that there is more to be said for the materialistic account of the universe than for the Christian. He sets aside the grave difficulties of materialism by labeling them with the phrase, "Insoluble question"; and for the rest he determines, like the pagan of old, "to snatch joyfully the gifts of the passing hour, and let alone the sterner aspects of life."

But it cannot be. Human nature is too great, even in its corruption, permanently to acquiesce in mere animalism; and his brute repose is disturbed from time to time by voices from a higher world, which echo, in plaintive agony, through the depths of his soul. At such times he would, he says, thankfully believe as Christians believe. But, then, he is not master of his convictions now; he cannot be. It is happier, he admits, to be a believer. But, then, he is a hero and martyr of skepticism; or he is a victim of necessities which he cannot control.

Ah, my brother! upon you too the star of the King of the Jews is shining, if you will but see it. There are facts of the spiritual world—such as your personality, your conscience, your free will—which your materialism cannot stamp out; which elude, in the last analysis, both the instruments of its anatomists and the logic of its dialecticians; and which, if you will only gaze persistently at any one of them, will reveal to you in all its beauty that world of spirit which exists alongside of, while it transcends, the world of matter. And of that spiritual world, Christ, and Christ alone, is King; of its mysterious problems, of its heights and depths, He alone is Master; so that as you cross the desert of inquiry which your one conviction, honestly pondered on, suggests, it shall lead you, like the star of old, to the cradle of the King of kings; and you too shall say in the end, "I have seen His star in the East, and am come to worship Him."

Or, here is a man who has fallen into bad company. He has lost all hold on what he once knew of the laws of God, and even of the laws of man. He utters blasphemy hour after hour with the punctilious regularity that governs the courtesies of good society. And as he wills not to retain God in his knowledge, God seems to have given him over, for the time, to a reprobate mind. To him sin is a trade in which he sees nothing to condemn except the unskilfulness which may bring it under the strong arm of the law. To him sin is an enthusiasm; he is the propagandist and apostle of unrighteousness; he is a very crusader against morality and truth; he works all uncleanness with greediness.

This, you will say, is an exaggeration. Would that it were an exaggeration: it is hard matter of fact. Between such an one as this, and the souls who love and worship our Divine Redeemer, there is an almost countless number of characters in whom light and darkness are blended in varying proportions. Yet the veriest profligate has his opportunity sooner or later; some word, some example, some passing inward aspiration, may be his star in the East, if he only will. Doubtless, to cross the desert is for him no easy matter; he has to break with habit, to resist weakness, to be deaf to ridicule. These things are hard for flesh and blood. Yet there it shines, the star of the King, bidding him hope and persevere; and everything depends, after the grace which has visited and is yet with him, upon his perseverance. Surely, when in moments of weakness he fears that all must give way, and that he must sink back into the darkness from which he is struggling forth towards the day, there is heard within him an assurance to which the outward encouragement is a welcome countersign: "Fear not: for I have redeemed thee, I have called thee by thy name; thou art Mine. When thou passest through the waters, I will be with thee; and through the rivers, they shall not overflow thee: when thou walkest through the fire, thou shalt not be burned; neither shall the flame kindle upon thee."

The Real Object of Our Search

A last lesson which this history teaches us is the real object of religious inquiry. "We have seen His star in the East, and are come to worship Him." Even Herod, insincere as he was, could not but adopt a language which imposed itself upon his natural conscience, when he bade the sages continue their journey: "When ye have found Him, bring me word again, that I may come and worship Him also."

Accordingly, we are told that "when they were come into the house, they saw the young Child with Mary His mother, and fell down and worshiped Him: and when they had opened their treasures, they presented unto Him gifts; gold, and frankincense, and myrrh."

In our day a great deal of use is made of the phrase, "religious thought." We hear of the forms of religious thought, the progress of religious thought, the development of religious thought, the results of religious thought; as if religion was preeminently, if not essentially, thought; as if a religious man was before all things else a thinker; as if when he had reached certain speculative conclusions all was well, for time and for eternity.

Nor may we deny that a religious man, especially if his understanding has been trained and exercised, will be a thoughtful man. He is bound to use his thought as well as, or rather beyond, his other faculties, to God's honor and glory. He can scarcely, if he would, decline exercising thought upon that one Object, compared with Whom all else is insignificant. It is impossible that when such great themes as God, eternity, the soul, life and death, have opened out upon his mind, he should not think of them often and deeply, if he is capable of thought at all. But this is a very different thing from saying that the exercise of thought is the essential thing in religion. For Holy Scripture and the Church represent the objects of religious thought as fixed, occupying a definite area, on the highest authority, and quite as much beyond the control and manipulation of human thought as are the sun or the fixed stars, although suggesting boundless matter for adoring contemplation.

Indeed, according to Holy Scripture, the essence of religion is not so much thought as practice. "Pure religion and undefiled before God and the Father is this, To visit the fatherless and the widows in their affliction, and to keep himself unspotted from the world." In point of fact, thought is one side of the religious action of the soul, or of the action of the Holy Spirit within the soul, while practice is the other. Thought without practice soon becomes an irreligious philosophy, and practice without thought a soulless mechanism.

Here the question arises, What is the meeting-point
between thought and practice? What is the act, if there be
any act, in which thought learns to be practical, and in
which practice gains strength, motive, intensity, by
copartnership with thought? I answer, Worship. For
worship is the joint result of thought and affection and
will, simultaneously rising towards God, and then sinking
into the dust before Him. There is no such thing as
worship, without thought, on the one hand, realizing its
Object; and affection and will, on the other, rescuing
thought from wasting away into thin, profitless, perhaps
irreverent, speculation, by embracing that Object. And
this is why worship so fructifies and strengthens the soul;
why it is, in fact, the central and representative act of the
soul's religious, that is, its true and highest, life. It is
much more than mere religious thought; it is the stimulant
and guide of religious practice. It is the soul, with all its
powers, seeking the true Center of the spiritual universe;
it is the soul realizing the original Source, the destined
End, and the present Object of its existence, by an act so
comprehensive as to enlist all its faculties, so intense as
to tax them when enlisted, even to the uttermost.

Thus it was that when the Wise Men had found Him to
Whom the star had guided them, they fell down and
worshiped Him. They fell down. They did not sit up, as if
nothing great was before them; or on the foolish supposition
that the body has no relation to the soul, and that while
the soul is cleaving unto the dust before the Majesty of
God, there is no reason why the body should not lounge
and loll on a chair in a posture of easy, if not of studied,
indifference. They fell down and worshiped; the outward
act corresponding to, and being dictated by, the inward
self-prostration, just as the Hebrew word for adoration
implies the prostration of the adoring soul.

Say you that this prostration was only Oriental? Was it
not rather profoundly human, and should we not do well
to note it? Ah! brethren, methinks we have much to learn
of these Eastern sages; we who, like them, come into the
presence of the King of kings, but who, unlike them, think
it perhaps proof of a high spirituality to behave before

Him as we should not think of behaving in the presence of our earthly superiors. Do we murmur that God looks not at the bowed head or at the bent knee, but at the heart? No doubt He does look at the heart; but the question is whether it is possible for the heart to be engaged in worship while the posture of the body suggests irreverent sloth.

Burke has shown, what must be apparent to every man of reflection and sense, that between the postures of the body and the emotions of the soul there is an intimate correspondence. You cannot, as a matter of physical fact, feel a sinner's self-abasement before the Sanctity of God, while you stretch yourself out in a chair with your arms crossed, and your eyes gazing listlessly at any object that may meet them. Doubtless the old and the weak may worship without prostrations, to which their bodies are no longer equal. For the young and strong to attempt this is to trifle not merely with the language of Scripture, but with the laws of our composite nature.

Be sure, brethren, that irreverence is not a note of spirituality. Reverence is the true language of faith, which sees God and adores Him. Irreverence is the symptom of unbelief or of indifference. When the soul's eye is closed to the Magnificence of God, the outward actions of worship are barely endured or contemptuously rejected as though they were lifeless forms.

But there was much more than this reverent outward homage in the worship of those Eastern sages. They proved their sincerity by their gifts; "gold, and frankincense, and myrrh." These were material symbols of things yet more precious; of His Sovereignty, His Godhead, His Sufferings; of their love, their piety, their self-denial. Their iniquity ended in discovery; and when they had found Christ, they did not curiously examine Him as if He was the solution of an intellectual puzzle; they worshiped Him as their King and their God. We may look on the material sun, in his brightness or in his eclipse, as day by day we learn to know more of him, and our highest knowledge ever stops at the stage of intelligent wonder; for this sun is but a creature, after all, and he only reflects the glory of that

Uncreated and awful Being Who made him. But at the Feet of the Sun of the moral world, of the Sun of Righteousness, it is, it must be, otherwise. At His Feet we have reached the very frontier and source of being; and to gaze without worship—true, inward, utter self-prostration before Him—is to deny the truth of what our spirits see.

May He grant to each of us who needs it at this blessed season, some star of His Epiphany, some tongue of fire that comes from Heaven; and may we watch until we follow it; and follow it, though amid discouragements, yet perseveringly, until we find Him, Whose messenger and evangelist it is!

Oh! send out Thy light and Thy truth, Eternal Jesus, and bring us, at this blessed season, unto Thy holy hill and to Thy dwelling; and we will go, in this our pilgrimage through time, to the Altar of God, even unto the God of our joy and gladness; and, through Thy grace and mercy, in the eternity beyond, upon the harp will we give thanks unto Thee, O Lord our God.

The Christmas Miracle

Clovis Gillham Chappell (1882-1972) was an American Methodist preacher. He was an eloquent evangelist and a popular public speaker. Chappell published many books of popular sermons and specialized in biblical character studies. This sermon is taken from *Living Zestfully*, published in 1944 by Abingdon-Cokesbury Press.

Clovis Gillham Chappell

13

THE CHRISTMAS MIRACLE

> In the beginning was the Word, and the Word was with God, and the Word was God. . . . And the Word was made flesh, and dwelt among us, and we beheld his glory. . . . No man hath seen God at any time; the only begotten Son, which is in the bosom of the Father, he hath declared him (John 1:1, 14, 18).

A CAREFUL READING of the opening chapter of the Fourth Gospel will indicate that these three verses belong together. The others are in a sense parenthetical. "In the beginning was the Word . . . and the Word was made flesh." This assertion takes us back across the far spaces of the years to the wonderful birth at Bethlehem. Not only so, but it takes us infinite distances beyond that birth into the timeless eternities. "In the beginning," says the author, using the majestic language of Genesis—"In the beginning was the Word, and the Word was with God, and the Word was God." This verb "was" is in the imperfect tense. It indicates not a single past act but one that took place continuously. "In the beginning was the Word continuously, and the Word was continuously with God, and the Word continuously was God. And the Word became flesh," a single act, "and dwelt among us, and we beheld his glory." Thus the writer brings us face to face with the miracle of Christmas.

The Humanity and Uniqueness of Jesus

"The Word was made flesh and dwelt among us." The author here is making a twofold affirmation:

1. He is asserting the humanity of Jesus. The fact that the Word became flesh means that the humanity of Jesus was just as real as that of ourselves. He came as a little baby even as you and I. He was nursed at a mother's

breast. He grew as we grew. He had to learn as we learn. He was subject to all our limitations. He became weary as we become weary. He slept as we sleep. He was sometimes perplexed as we are perplexed. He was tempted as we are tempted. At last he died, passing through the same grim experience through which we ourselves must one day pass. To forget or to question the humanity of Jesus is to fall into the first heresy that vexed the Christian Church. The first heresy was not a questioning of the unique divinity of Jesus. It was a doubting of his humanity.

To rob Jesus of his humanity is to empty the incarnation of its meaning. If Jesus was not as human as we are, then the most helpful life that was ever lived ceases to be a help. Take the matter of his temptation, for instance. If he was not truly human, then his temptation was a sham battle. He was play-acting in his conflict with the devil. Naturally he could go bravely to such battle. He knew he was invulnerable. But such is not the case with me. I know that in this battle I may lose. I know I am capable of being wounded to death. Since Jesus was truly man, the same was true of him. He was tempted in all points like as we are. He had the same capacity to fall. Therefore, "in that he himself hath suffered being tempted, he is able to succor them that are tempted." Jesus was truly human.

2. The second affirmation of this text is that in the coming of Jesus, God came in a unique sense to dwell among men. This great assertion of the Fourth Gospel does not stand alone. It is in harmony with the Bible as a whole. The greatest prophets of the Old Testament dreamed of a good day when God should break into human life in a unique fashion. They were sure that, sometime, somehow, God was going to come to show man the way home. The New Testament shows us this dream as an accomplished reality. In truth, it was the conviction that God had come in the flesh that gave birth to the New Testament. Without this Christmas miracle not a single page of the Gospels nor a single page of the Epistles would have been written. It was just this conviction of the divine Lordship of Jesus that gave birth to the Christian

Church. These first followers of Jesus were pronounced monotheists to a man. Yet they went out to proclaim the Lordship of Jesus as a fundamental fact of their faith.

How did they come by this revolutionary conviction? They learned it from Jesus himself. He convinced them both by what he was and by what he said, by his life and by his lips. Unique in himself, he was unique in his teaching. He did not, as other teachers, point away from himself to the truth. He said, rather, "I am the truth." He did not merely claim to show men the way to God; he said, "I am the way." He did not merely point men to the springs of living water; he said, "I am the water of life." When other teachers asked questions that they thought fundamental, they put their questions in this fashion: "What think ye of my doctrine?" But when Jesus asked the question that he thought fundamental, he asked, "What think ye of Christ?" "Whom do men say that I am?" When Peter answered this question by saying, "Thou art the Christ, the Son of the living God," Jesus did not rebuke him. He said, rather, "Blessed art thou, Simon, son of Jonah: for flesh and blood hath not revealed it unto thee, but my Father which is in heaven." Jesus declared further that the destinies of men and of nations, both for time and eternity, depended upon their attitude toward him. When, therefore, John affirms that in the coming of Jesus, God came in a unique sense, he is speaking in harmony with the Bible as a whole and with the Christian Church.

What Did His Coming Accomplish?

What beneficent results did the Word accomplish by becoming flesh? Let me mention four:

1. The Word became flesh in order to bring to man an adequate revelation of God. "No man hath seen God at any time; the only begotten Son, which is in the bosom of the Father, he hath declared him." The Christmas miracle is essentially good news about God. The great seers and saints of mankind had known much of God before Jesus came. One cannot read the Shepherd Psalm without a realization of that fact. They had seen something of his

power in nature. They had seen something of his beauty in the faces of the best men and women they had known. But a more adequate revelation was needed. God remains an abstraction to most of us until we see him in terms of personality.

This is true of so many weighty words! When I was preparing this sermon, I turned to Webster's International Dictionary in quest of definitions of some of the great words. First, I wanted to know what light is. I found out. "It is the essential condition of vision, an emanation from a light-giving body." How thrilling! When I read it, I was eager to tuck that heavy book under my arm and hurry out to read that definition to every person I knew. No, that was not the case at all. I knew that one glimpse of a glowworm would be worth more for the understanding of light than all the definitions in the world.

Then I looked up "life." I found that definition so stale and flat that, were it all that I knew about life, I would hardly care to live. When I looked up the word "God," the results were little better. This is the case because there is no putting the Eternal God into a definition. We may get glimpses of him in nature. We find something of his beauty in the faces of the saints. But we see him adequately only in Jesus. By this we are not affirming that we see all of God even in Jesus. In taking upon himself the nature of man, Paul tells us, Jesus emptied himself. But while we do not see all of God in Jesus, we see all that our human nature can reveal and all that our human hearts need. When we see him bend in mercy over publicans and harlots, when we see him gather little children in his arms, when we hear him pray in the midst of the agonies of the cross, "Father, forgive them; for they know not what they do," we can ask nothing better even of the infinite God than that he be like this Man who lived and died for others.

2. It is through the Incarnation that Jesus reveals us to ourselves. He is not only a revelation of God; he is a revelation of man. In his presence we become conscious of our moral failure. But Jesus not only shows us what we are; he shows us also what we may become. He is a

revelation of our amazing possibilities. In his presence we believe in "The Land of Beginning Again." He makes us sure that even a fluctuating son of Jonah can become a rock of Christ-like character. You remember that brilliant young genius who stood years ago before a canvas of Titian. As this young man looked at the work of that great master, his cheeks took on a new glow, his eyes sparkled, and he said to himself, "I, too, Titian! I, too, am a painter." And as men through the centuries have looked at Jesus, they have said, "I, too, O Lord and Master! I, too, may live sacrificially and worthfully."

3. Then Jesus by his Incarnation shows us what is to be our relationship both to God and to each other. Our relationship to God is to be that of sons. When we pray, we are to say, "Our Father." Our relationship to each other is to be that of brothers. It was this relationship that Jesus made visible before our eyes. He summed up in himself that kingdom of right relationships which he called the Kingdom of heaven or the Kingdom of God. It is for this Kingdom that we are made. It is the laws of this Kingdom that we are to obey. Here is the way we are to live our lives. Here is where we fit in. To live after this fashion is to live abundantly. To live in any other way is to find not life but death. This is not theory; it is experience.

4. Finally, in Jesus we not only see God's first revelation of himself and of the Kingdom of right relationships into which we are to enter, but in him we find the power for realization. Today, as in the long ago, this is true: "As many as received him, to them gave he power to become the sons of God." We do not have to coax Jesus into our lives; we have only to receive him. By receiving him we come to share his nature. By receiving him we enter his Kingdom and come to share his attitude toward God and man. By receiving him we come to share his power to heal a wounded world. "He that believeth on me, the works that I do shall he do also." If we permit him to be born within us today, we shall have in a real sense the Christmas spirit. This is true because in receiving Jesus we receive God.

How Can We Be Sure?

How can we believe this? How can we of today be sure that in the coming of Jesus, God came in a unique sense to dwell among men? Naturally, we pass by certain arguments that appealed strongly to our fathers. They found it easier to believe in Jesus because of his unique birth. But this argument makes little appeal to the man of today. It is something that we cannot prove. Personally, I accept the virgin birth, but my sole reason for doing so is that I believe in Jesus. It is Jesus who makes his unique birth credible.

How then, I repeat, can we believe that Jesus was divine in a unique sense? I offer the following suggestions that have been helpful to me:

1. I believe that Jesus was divine in a unique sense because he was possessed of a unique character. Jesus was the one Man of all the ages who was not a sinner. He was more than sinless; he was incarnate goodness. This is unique. When we hear Paul say, "There is no difference: for all have sinned, and come short of the glory of God," we say, "Amen." Even if we are not conscious of positive wrongdoing, we are conscious of falling short of our highest possibilities. We have neither been our best nor done our best. If the best man we know were to say to us, "Not once have I done wrong; not once has duty knocked at my door and failed to find me in," such a word would discredit that man. In fact, there is almost nothing that he could say that would offend us so deeply. Yet here is One of whom it is written that he "knew no sin," and this high assertion does not offend us. The impression that the Gospels leave on the overwhelming majority is that here is the story of a perfect Man.

But how may we know that these evangelists were not creating this perfection out of their own imaginations? For the simple reason that they could not. If the greatest genius of our day were to undertake to draw a perfect character, the perfection of that character might not be your idea of perfection at all. Were he to create a character that would appeal to our whole generation as perfect, that character might not make the same appeal to those of another generation. Then it is evident that the writers of the Gospels were not trying to draw a perfect character. They were simply seeking to record the facts. Yet the impression that these records have left upon the centuries is that it is the story of a Man who was without flaw.

Even more impressive than the claims made for Jesus are the claims that he made for himself. This Man was so sensitive to sin that he rebuked sin in others as none other that ever lived. This Man who declared that it was better to cut off the right hand and to pluck out the right eye than to do the guilty thing he proclaimed himself not guilty. "Which of you," he asked, "convicteth me of sin?" When he stood at the end of the way, when he stood in the immediate presence of death and the immediate presence of God, at that solemn hour when the most flippant become serious, when, if ever, we are honest, he claimed perfection. Speaking to his Father, he used these great words: "I have glorified thee on the earth: I have finished the work which thou gavest me to do." Thus he claimed not merely to have reached the end of his life but to have finished it, to have brought it to perfection. He had left nothing undone that he ought to have done. He had left no tear undried that he ought to have dried, no burden unlifted that he might have lifted; nor had he planted a single thorn that he would like now to pluck up. His is the one perfect life that our world has known.

If you are minded to argue that Jesus was misquoted, that he never made these high claims for himself, then I answer that what he said by his whole attitude is quite as impressive as what he is credited with saying with his lips. Here, I repeat, is a Man who was an incarnate conscience to everyone who really saw him. In his presence honest Simon Peter fell upon his knees and cried: "Depart from me; for I am a sinful man, O Lord." A hardened highwayman who died at his side looked at him and sobbed out this confession: "I am suffering justly, but this man hath done nothing amiss."

To this day he rebukes us as none other that ever lived. Yet he who so rebuked sin in others never once, so far as the record goes, showed the slightest consciousness of sin in himself. Never once was he penitent. He taught all others to pray, "Forgive us our trespasses"; but never once did he seek forgiveness. Never once did he show the slightest grief for a single act nor lament a single failure. The whole impression, I repeat, that Jesus makes to this day is that he was sinless.

To undertake to explain this fact by saying that Jesus was the best man who ever lived is simply no explanation at all. This is the case because those who are most tormented by a sense of guilt are not the worst of men but the best. When we listen to confessions red with shame, they come, as a rule, not from the lips of the great sinners but from the lips of the great saints. "Now Job was a perfect man," is the beginning of that majestic drama called by his name. In the presence of his friends he stoutly maintained his integrity. But by and by when he had a vision of God all was changed: "I have heard of thee by the hearing of the ear: but now mine eye seeth thee. Wherefore I abhor myself, and repent in dust and ashes." But here is One whom all acknowledge to be good. Yet this good Man never showed the slightest penitence even in the presence of God. We believe, therefore, that he was more than good—that he was perfect.

> "Oh, what amiss may I forgive in Thee,
> Jesus, good Paragon, thou Crystal Christ?"

2. I believe that Jesus was divine in a unique sense because, though crucified nineteen hundred years ago, he is still a living presence among us. He is what another has called "Our Eternal Contemporary." That which gave the saints of the Early Church their amazing joy and power was the consciousness of his presence. That which steadied them when all human help failed was his nearness. "At my first answer no man stood with me, but all men forsook me: I pray God that it may not be laid to their charge. Notwithstanding the Lord stood with me, and strengthened me; that by me the preaching might be fully known . . . and I was delivered out of the mouth of the lion." These early saints had an optimism, a dauntless

courage, that made fear impossible. This was the case because they were sure that they were not alone. They were convinced out of their own experiences that their Lord was making good his promise, "Lo, I am with you alway, even unto the end of the world."

This experience of the early saints has been the experience of the saints of every age. Here is a man, J. G. Paton by name, who is burying his wife and baby at the midnight hour in far-off Hebrides. No scene could be more lonely, few ordeals more trying. How does he manage to see it through? This is his own answer: "The ever-merciful Lord sustained me to lay the precious dust of my loved ones in the same quiet grave. But for Jesus, and the fellowship He vouchsafed me there, I must have gone mad and died beside that lonely grave!" Here is another man, my close personal friend. He passed recently "to where beyond these voices there is peace." He suffered from a disease that was tragic in the extreme. Yet he remained more than serene. There was a radiance in his face that was never seen on land or sea. What was his secret? He told it to me one day in these words: "Jesus Christ is as real to me as my own right hand." I can, therefore, believe in his unique divinity because, though crucified, he still lives. He is still face to face with every soul who is willing to recognize him.

3. But these, to the unbeliever, are only evidences. Evidences, however helpful, are not enough. The faith that Jesus is a living presence may become a conviction of the mind; but before we call him Lord, something else is needed. We must obey him. This is the road to certainty, and the only road. In so saying, I am not stating something that is unique. How do we know that honey is sweet? Only by tasting it. How do we know the thrill of love? Only by loving. How do we come to say, "My Lord and my God"? Only by obeying. "If any one," said Jesus, "is willing to do His will, he shall know."

Are you eager to make this Christmas miracle personal to yourself? If so, I offer you this simple direction: Begin here and now the best you know to do the will of Jesus. Follow the light that you have, and that light will become brighter and brighter until you come to certainty. This is the open road to personal victory, but it is more—it is the open road to the highest type of usefulness. If you give yourself to this present Christ today, he will give himself to you. As he gives himself to you, you will have both a new passion and a new power to give to a needy world. By thus yielding, you will be able to do in some measure what Jesus did in the long ago—make God real to men.